Risk Management in Software Development Projects

For my two sons, Sean and Timothy

Risk Management in Software Development Projects

John McManus

Routledge
Taylor & Francis Group

LONDON AND NEW YORK

First published 2004 by Butterworth-Heinemann

This edition published 2011 by Routledge
2 Park Square, Milton Park, Abingdon, Oxfordshire OX14 4RN
711 Third Avenue, New York, NY 10017, USA

First issued in hardback 2016

Routledge is an imprint of the Taylor & Francis Group, an informa business

British Library Cataloguing in Publication Data
A catalogue record for this book is available from the British Library

ISBN 13: 978-1-138-15174-1 (hbk)
ISBN 13: 978-0-7506-5867-6 (pbk)

Contents

Computer Weekly Professional Series

There are few professions which require as much continuous updating as that of the IS executive. Not only does the hardware and software scene change relentlessly, but also ideas about the actual management of the IS function are being continuously modified, updated and changed. Thus keeping abreast of what is going on is really a major task.

Computer Weekly Professional Series has been created to assist IS executives keep up-to-date with the management ideas and issues of which they need to be aware.

One of the key objectives of the series is to reduce the time it takes for leading edge management ideas to move from the academic and consulting environments into the hands of the IT practitioner. Thus this series employs appropriate technology to speed up the publishing process. Where appropriate some books are supported by CD-ROM or by additional information or templates located on the Web.

This series provides IT professionals with an opportunity to build up a bookcase of easily accessible, but detailed information on the important issues that they need to be aware of to successfully perform their jobs.

Aspiring or already established authors are invited to get in touch with me directly if they would like to be published in this series.

Dr Dan Remenyi
Series Editor
dan.remenyi@mcil.co.uk

Other titles in the Series
Corporate politics for IT managers: how to get streetwise
Delivering IT and e-business value
eBusiness implementation
eBusiness strategies for virtual organizations
The effective measurement and management of IT costs and benefits
ERP: the implementation cycle
A hacker's guide to project management
How to become a successful IT consultant
How to manage the IT helpdesk
Information warfare: corporate attack and defence in a digital world
IT investment – making a business case
Knowledge management – a blueprint for delivery
Make or break issues in IT management
Making IT count
Network security
Prince 2: a practical handbook
The project manager's toolkit
Reinventing the IT department
Understanding the Internet

Preface

A recent paper by the author, 'Risk in Software Projects' (in *Management Services*, October 2001), briefly referred to risk mitigation and its role in the risk management process. Publication of this paper prompted considerable discussion and requests for further information, particularly on software projects in the design phase. My ongoing work into risk management since that paper was originally published has resulted in the development of a risk management tool/ methodology for software projects. This has also provided the impetus to produce a more complete integrated methodology, providing a basis for all the risk analysis material in this book.

In writing this book I was conscious of the need to bridge a gap between current theory and what is good practice in the management of software development projects. The book aims to do this by focusing on what the practitioner needs to know about risk in the pursuit of delivering software projects.

The book is structured into six chapters. Chapters 2–5 are dedicated to a specific element of the risk model (or paradigm). Chapter 1 sets the framework for Chapters 2–5. Each chapter ends with a self-assessment checklist, and the subsequent chapter starts with a recap on the previous one. Chapter 6 is entirely devoted to a case study. Whilst I have attempted to refrain from duplication, some duplication within chapters is inevitable. However, I believe that this helps the reader by reinforcing the points made in previous chapters.

Where appropriate to do so, I have used the terms 'software project manager' and 'project manager' interchangeably throughout the book. In essence, however, they are the same entity.

Any book of this type can be improved upon and so I would welcome any feedback you may have via the publisher. I trust you enjoy reading this book.

John McManus

Acknowledgements

Books of this type are rarely written in a vacuum – indeed the most successful practitioner books are the product of people's work experiences. *Risk Management in Software Development Projects* is no exception.

First, I would like to acknowledge those practitioners and academics who provided advice and material to me in the preparation of this text – their contributions are sincerely appreciated. I am especially indebted to: Dr David Brewer and Dr Michael Nash of Gamma Secure Systems Limited; Dr Karl E. Wiegers of Process Impact; Dr James Collofello, Arizona State University; Dr Robert Charette, President ITABHI Corporation; Will Ozier (Institute of Internal Auditors, USA); David McNamee, of MC^2 Management Consulting; John Desmond, Editorial Director of *Software Magazine*, Wiesner Publishing, USA; Karen Gibson, Copyright Department, Blackwell Publishers Oxford, UK; and Sarah Strauss, Copyright Department, Software Engineering Institute, USA. I would also like to thank Nick Wheldon, of Mitchell-Beazley Publishers, for his assistance in locating the distribution agent for Paul Harrison's book *Operational Research – Core Business Studies*.

I acknowledge the assistance of my partner Jennifer, who did much of the proof-reading and offered some valuable advice in the preparation of Chapter 1, and provided the due diligence effort in reading various drafts of the manuscript.

Finally, I would like to express my thanks and gratitude to the Editorial and Production team at Elsevier Butterworth-Heinemann, especially Mike Cash, Jennifer Wilkinson, Deena Burgess, and Deborah Puleston for their hard work in getting this project off the ground.

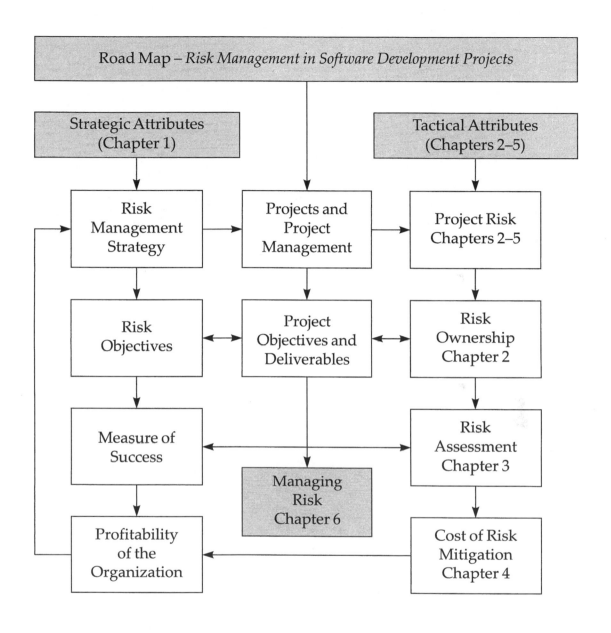

The risk management process

1.1 Introduction to software risk management

Project management and software engineering is the technical and managerial discipline concerned with the systematic invention, production, and maintenance of high quality software products delivered on time, at minimum cost. Given this statement, in this decade of the twenty-first century the complexity of the marketplace, the rapid change in technologies and the global shortage of skilled IT staff place unprecedented business risks on customers and suppliers alike. To emphasize this point, in 1985 the worldwide software costs were €140 billion; in 1995, this figure had risen to €450 billion at a growth rate of 12 per cent per year. The projected expenditure is estimated to be €1400 billion by 2005.

Given this situation, global IT software suppliers and system integration organizations face challenges like never before. The global IT software industry stands to lose billions each year in project overruns, and reworking software. In my experience, as much as 40 per cent of software development costs alone can be spent reworking software, and on a global scale this represents a tidy sum. Furthermore, on average only one in six software projects will be delivered on time and to budget, and in some large organizations only 10 per cent of their projects will come in on time and to budget. Even when these projects are completed, many are no more than a mere shadow of their original application requirements.

These claims are substantiated by the historical research undertaken by the Standish Group (survey in 1995) representing 8380 software application projects. They produced the following results:

- Challenged projects: 53 per cent were completed but incurred cost and schedule overruns, resulting in fewer features than originally specified.
- Cancelled projects: 31 per cent of projects were cancelled at some time during the development cycle.
- The average cost of overrun for challenged and cancelled projects was 190 per cent of the original cost estimate.
- The average schedule overrun for challenged and cancelled projects was 222 per cent of the original estimate.
- On average, challenged projects were delivered with only 31 per cent of the originally specified features and functions.

Research would support that projects usually fail because of management mistakes rather than technical mistakes and it could be argued that managerial issues are more important than technical issues in software engineering projects. Figure 1.1 outlines some major causes of project failure.

Managerial issues – account for 65 per cent of failure

- Inappropriate project structure and channels of communication
- Inappropriate resources (poor skill and knowledge mix)
- Inappropriate estimates
- Inappropriate planning methods (poor scheduling and tracking)
- Inappropriate user buy-in
- Inappropriate risk management

Technical issues – account for 35 per cent of failure

- Inappropriate software requirements
- Inappropriate technical design
- Inappropriate development and testing tools
- Inappropriate technical documentation
- Inappropriate technical support
- Inappropriate technical reviews (and quality audits)

Figure 1.1
Major causes of project failure

Although these statistics on project failures may be alarming they are in essence symptoms of poor or inadequate project and risk management.

1.1.1 Defining risk

The term software risk management can mean different things to many different people, in considering what is meant by risk we need to understand the qualitative, quantitative and philosophical aspects of what constitutes risk. There are numerous definitions on what constitutes risk; however, since this book is about risk in software development projects I offer the reader two definitions:

A simple definition of a 'risk' is a problem that could cause some loss or threaten the success of our project, but which hasn't happened yet. These potential problems might have an adverse impact on the cost, schedule, or technical success of the project, the quality of our software products, or project team morale. Risk management is the process of identifying, addressing, and eliminating these potential problems before they can damage our project.

(Wiegers 1998)

Alternatively:

Risk is a combination of an abnormal event or failure and the consequences of that event or failure to a system's operators, users or environment. A risk can range from catastrophic (loss of an entire system; loss of life or permanent disability) to negligible (no system damage or injury).

(Glutch 1994)

Although different in context, what these definitions have in common is that uncertainty, failure and adversity can lead to catastrophe and losses. In other words not understanding what constitutes risk and how to manage risk is bad news for everyone.

Threats to software projects usually result from some unknown quantity. For example, external influences such as different stakeholder groups who are usually associated with high degrees of managerial risk. External threats to projects pose real issues for project managers and their teams especially where political influence is brought to bear, for instance, in cases of funding or appointments to project boards.

In considering external threats it is perhaps important to note the extent to which any such pressures are associated with industry dynamics, an important consideration in organizations that are competing for projects. Michael Porter has developed a model for evaluating external threats. This model is known as the five forces model.

The concept behind the model involves a relationship between competitors within an industry, potential competitors, suppliers, buyers and alternative solutions to the problem being addressed. Whilst the model was originally developed as a strategy tool it can be adapted for use in analysing macro level risk and external threats. In general, the greater the pressure from potential entrants or substitute products or services, the less attractive the project and the greater the threat. The threat of software related losses should provide a significant incentive to businesses to manage the risks of essential project failure. Amongst software integrators competition to win major project business is ferocious and for many involves a high degree of risk certainly where software products are concerned (Figure 1.2). At an industry level such threats (risks) will include those identified in Figure 1.3.

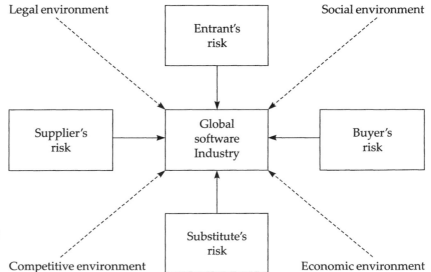

Figure 1.2
Global software industry (adapted from Porter 1985)

If not examined at the outset the threats listed in Figure 1.3 usually end up downstream as major causes of project failure. A few years ago I happened to run a workshop on risk for several senior managers contemplating the introduction of a new software product. During discussions, it became apparent that several of the participants held naïve attitudes towards risk management. Some of the clearest indicators of project maturity are to be found in attitudes to risk. Managers who see dialogue

Business	Technological
• Pricing strategy	• Production limitations
• Legal restrictions (litigation)	• Design compatibility
• Potential for copying	• Production limitations
• Payments and royalties	• Degree of innovation
• Potential for customer participation	• Proprietary technology
• Timing of introduction	• Patent(s)
• Stakeholder influence	• Technology uniqueness

Figure 1.3
Some threats to industry-wide software projects

on risk as being negative reveal not only a non-professional attitude but also complete ignorance about the nature of the environment in which projects are managed and delivered. The story also illustrates that the decision whether to take a risk is affected by the surrounding circumstances. In a project setting numerous functionaries may be weighing the pluses and minuses. But once a risk is taken the project manager has a distinct role in handling, eliminating or modifying conditions that can make the risk go out of kilter.

1.2 Why do we need to manage risk in software development projects?

The simplest answer to this question is that if we do not then the organization loses money, the trust of its stakeholders, its reputation and perhaps it finally goes bust. The following examples show in no uncertain terms that software risk must be managed like other serious business risks:

- Hershey's sales for Q3 1999 – the company's peak shipping period – dropped more than $150 million (12 per cent) from the previous year because of an enterprise software glitch that prevented Halloween candy from being shipped. As a result, the candy maker's net income for that same period was down 19 per cent from 1998.
- Online auction giant eBay experienced a revenue loss of nearly $4 million in the form of customer credits when a software problem caused a 22-hour system outage in June 1999. The lost revenue was just the beginning of eBay's problems; the impact on investor confidence resulted in a loss of $5.7 billion in market capitalization.

- In 1999, the US Securities and Exchange Commission fielded over 20 000 investor complaints related to software problems in online trading – a dramatic increase from the roughly 1000 complaints filed in 1998.
- The former parent company of bankrupt pharmaceutical distributor FoxMeyer is suing SAP for $500 million because the vendor's enterprise resource planning software allegedly brought FoxMeyer to a virtual standstill.

(Goodwin 2000)

Clearly software mistakes are expensive and can lead to organizations going out of business. Prevention is always better than cure. At first glance, risk management might appear just to add complexity to an already complex undertaking. In reality, however, risk management activities make software projects less complex. For example:

- Identification and prioritization of risks enable project managers and project staff to focus on the areas with the most impact to their project.
- Appropriate risk mitigation actions reduce overall project risk thus accelerating project completion.
- Projects that finish sooner cost less, plus risk mitigation actions can further reduce project cost.
- Projects using software risk management have more predictable schedules; they experience fewer surprises, since they have identified risks before they can become problems.

Risk management doesn't necessarily mean avoiding projects that could incur a high level of risk. Prospering in today's software marketplace often means that high risk projects are precisely the ones we need to undertake. Formal risk management makes sure we go into such projects with our eyes open, so we know what kinds of things could go wrong, and we've done our best to make sure those factors won't prevent the ultimate success of the project.

1.2.1 Cost

Preparing a detailed risk assessment for a software project is costly and time consuming; however, in the long run the benefits that accrue normally outweigh the cost involved. Software risk management experts agree that the costs associated with taking a few preventative measures early on are negligible when compared to the dramatic costs that can be incurred when proper risk management techniques are neglected. Most importantly, companies should consider a software risk management insurance policy. It will cost more if you think about it after the fact rather than plan for it in advance. And remember, reducing the total cost of risk goes direct to the bottom line.

We need to balance such costs against the potential cost we could incur if the risk is not addressed and does indeed bite us. It may not be cost effective to reduce uncertainty too much. For example, if we are concerned about the ability of a subcontractor to deliver an essential component of our product on time, we could engage multiple subcontractors to increase the likelihood that at least one will come through on schedule. That's an expensive remedy for a problem that may not even exist. Is it worth it? It depends on the downside we incur if indeed the subcontractor dependency causes the project to miss its planned ship date. Only you can decide for each individual situation (Wiegers 1998).

1.2.2 Assessment

Of course some projects occasionally require a less rigorous assessment. Depending on the scope and size of the project, organizations may find it appropriate to remain with the initial risk assessment. In these circumstances a more in-depth risk assessment can be developed should the initial assessment indicate it is necessary.

1.3 Use of software risk management

Any organization has a fundamental role to play in the management of risk. Organizations are entrusted with shareholder funds, and therefore have a particular duty to observe the highest standards of governance. The organization must ensure that it has a sound system of internal management and control, and delivers value for money to its clients. The organization, however, is not responsible for the day-to-day management of risk, that is usually the project manager's job. In the context of risk management the organization should, as a minimum, ensure that there is an ongoing process for identifying, evaluating, and managing the risks faced by the establishment, and should review this process regularly.

Generally speaking, most organizations will wish to consider the most significant risks facing their establishment at appropriate intervals. The organization's job, therefore, is to:

1 Set the tone and influence the culture of risk management within the whole establishment. For example:
   - is it a 'risk taking' or 'risk averse' institution?
   - which types of risk are acceptable and which are not?
   - is the portfolio of risk suitably balanced between high risk/high return and low risk/low return?
   - what are the expectations of staff with respect to conduct and integrity?
   - is there a clear policy that describes the risk culture, defines scope and responsibilities, assesses resources and defines performance measures?
2 Determine the appropriate risk desire or level of exposure for the establishment:
   - for example, is a software project with a potential loss of 15 per cent of total income acceptable, or should the risk be spread by working with another organization or transferred through the use of insurance?
3 Actively participate in major decisions affecting the establishment risk profile or exposure:
   - for example, major financial investment and overseas partnerships.
4 Monitor the management of significant risks to reduce the likelihood of unwelcome surprises:
   - for example, by receiving regular reports from project management focusing on key performance and risk indicators (probably no more than 20), supplemented by audit and other internal and external reports.
5 Satisfy itself that the less significant risks are being actively managed, possibly by encouraging a wider adoption of risk management.
6 Report annually on the establishment approach to risk management, with a description of the key elements of its processes and procedures.

Research suggests that senior managers within the organization need to strike the right balance between keeping an overview and avoiding involvement in day-to-day management. Unfortunately there is not one single right approach in project terms; the need for a formal approach to project risk management is important because:

- It helps a delivery to focus on problem areas, ensuring that all potential problems are faced and solutions are documented
- It allows all personnel on a project to record their perception of what could go wrong and offer ideas on how to avoid or reduce the impact of such problems
- It provides an audit record of how risk has been considered on a project
- It helps the project manager set contingency budgets and then review the adequacy of these budgets as the delivery progresses.

Remember the use of risk management is easier to achieve in an organization that:

- Trusts teams to make major decisions
- Supports diversity in employees
- Supports and encourages professional development in staff
- Trains staff in problem solving, innovation, creativity, quality service and finding solutions
- Encourages individuals to accept direct responsibility for their area's activities and results and generates a sense of ownership
- Encourages team members to play different roles within the team on which they serve
- Encourages staff to move in and out of teams as their skills and knowledge are needed
- Encourages teams to seek input from other stakeholders throughout a process
- Does not assume that the organization's way is the only right way
- Welcomes new ideas and perspectives, regardless of who offers these insights
- Views disagreement as the basis for a more robust solution.

1.3.1 Approach

Although there are different schools of thought, my view is that the software project risk approach should address risk in a top-down, granular, periodic fashion, and concern high level decisions, such as whether a project should be initiated, should it receive funding, has it passed a major milestone, etc. Its primary focus is on understanding the risks (and opportunities) that exist before plans are defined and/or put into operation. Risk management practice, on the other hand, concentrates on performing bottom-up, detailed, continuous assessment of risk (and again opportunity), concerning itself with addressing the day-to-day operational risks that a project faces. Together they provide a 360 degree, three-dimensional view of the risk that might confront a project.

It is worthwhile stating at this point that both the management of risk and risk management approaches follow a repeatable and iterative process of assessment, that is the identification, estimation and evaluation of the risks confronting a project and management (the planning for, monitoring of, and controlling of the means to eliminate or reduce the likelihood or consequences of the risks discovered). Both take a holistic or systems view of the risks likely to be encountered from their own unique perspectives and likewise take a systems view of how they should be mitigated. Both should be done continually over the life of a project from its initiation to its completion. Finally, both should be performed not only by project managers, but also by team members, third party contractors working in conjunction and co-operation with the project team. At this level, open communication of risk is key to its successful management, a point we will address later.

1.3.2 Techniques

Developments in risk management techniques have allowed some software organizations to implement and strengthen their management of risk. Modelling techniques and thinking methods such as brainstorming have gained favour within project management. These thinking techniques are used to understand risk and include qualitative, semi-quantitative and quantitative techniques. These methods are frequently applied in the workplace by themselves or in conjunction with other techniques. Although not exhaustive, they include:

Qualitative methods:

- Brainstorming
- SWOT analysis
- Maps
- Checklists and questionnaires
- Peer interviews.

These five techniques and their application will be discussed in Chapter 2.

Quantitative methods:

- Symbolic models
- Probability analysis
- Consequence analysis
- Decision trees
- Monte Carlo analysis
- Borda voting method
- Investment decision making
- Cost benefit analysis
- Quantitative market research.

These techniques and their application will be discussed in Chapter 3.

1.4 Objectives and goals of software risk management

It was stated earlier that software risk must be managed like any other serious business risk. The objective is therefore to understand what constitutes risk and eliminate the possible occurrence of it becoming a threat or a major source of rework. In my experience one of the most common sources of friction between senior managers and software project managers is the fact that senior managers do not communicate the strategic intent on risk. For clarity I repeat what was stated earlier: the practice of software risk management includes both top-down and bottom-up perspectives.

The top-down objectives of software risk management can be summarized as follows:

- Purging or reduction of political risk
- Purging or reduction of economic risk
- Purging or reduction of business risk
- Purging or reduction of technical risk.

Every risk situation has an antidote, the question is: What can the organization best afford? Organizations need to be able to trade off the risk and remedy, accepting the one with the lesser long-term impact in terms of time, cost and quality upon the project. We need to evaluate the options in terms of their risks or the antidotes that the organization can establish. In essence the balance is struck between the organization's willingness to suffer the consequence of risk and its willingness to pay for its avoidance, and that balance will depend on the organization's wealth and aversion to risk.

In setting objectives for the management of software project risk, project managers are inclined to view risk from two major perspectives: the technological and the business viewpoints. The technological perspective identifies the development tools, techniques, implementation environment of the software and business impact, whereas the business perspective deals with the productivity, profit, performance, demand, budget, revenue and business case. Whilst software risk may be addressed from a business perspective, in many cases software risk management is not addressed from a political or strategic perspective. Whilst strategic and project risks are differentiated in the development of software, they must relate to each other and risk management should be structured across the software development life cycle in order to implement a risk management approach that meets overall business concerns.

1.4.1 Goals

If reducing the economic cost of risk is one of the primary objectives of the organization risk management policy then the goals of risk management are all elements that constitute an approach to prevention. For example, let's assume that the cost of risk for a specified software development project is the total value of all related costs and resources, both direct and indirect. The total cost of risk to an organization is the sum of the following:

- Lost productivity (failure to meet contractual milestones and key deliverables)
- The replacement value of all software and hardware
- Expenditures, including any legal expenditures
- The costs of loss prevention and control measures
- The costs of insurance premiums (if applicable)
- Administrative and overhead costs.

Since reduction of the economic cost of risk is the primary objective of our risk management agenda, specific goals that support this primary objective are to:

- Minimize exposures to financial losses (contractual and other)
- Protect physical and software assets

- Reduce frequency and severity of errors
- Provide a reasonably safe environment for employees
- Minimize client changes and interruptions during development.

In setting objectives the usual practice is to quantify your objective. The metric you choose for your objective should directly reflect your organization's goals as defined in Figure 1.4. Thus, metrics are used to define success. If your goal is reduced economic risk on software projects, then metrics will measure your progress to that goal, see Figure 1.4. Metrics will also help you to understand some of the trade-offs you may face to reach those goals. A point to remember, however, is that collecting random metrics is a waste of everyone's time. A good way to determine appropriate metrics for your organization is to use the Goal, Question and Metric approach:

- Identify your goals (organizational and project)
- Determine what questions need to be answered to achieve those goals
- Determine what metrics you can collect to answer those questions.

1.4.2 Goals v. capability

The capability of an organization's internal process helps to predict a project's ability to manage risk and meet its goals.

Organizational objective Reduce economic risk on all major software projects	Goal 1	Goal 2	Goal 3
Measure Cost reduction on software development 20 per cent by June 2003	Minimize exposure to financial losses	Reduce frequency and severity of errors	Minimize client changes and interruptions during development
Owner Head of Software Development			
Stakeholder group Project managers			

Figure 1.4 Objective v. goal summary

Consequently projects in low capability organizations experience wide variations in achieving cost, functionality, and quality targets. Without question when it comes to delivering software projects organizations of low capability suffer the highest incidence of failure.

1.5 Developing a software risk management strategy

As suggested previously risk management creates value because the savings it produces will go direct to the bottom line. This contribution (savings in the organization's cost of risk) usually requires some investment linked to an overall risk management strategy.

A risk management strategy should identify the strategic aims of the organization (and its projects) and create a blueprint for futureproofing the business. For example, one, software engineering company I worked for identified its strategic aims as:

- Integrating software risk management into the company culture
- Raising awareness and knowledge transfer
- Articulating responsibilities and structure for managing software risk
- Providing standard terminology for software risk management
- Compliance with agreed standards and procedures.

Anchored to these aims were the following objectives:

- To ensure the company fulfils its role
- To preserve and enhance the company's reputation with its clients
- To protect the assets and interests of the company
- To protect the interests of its staff
- To implant the concepts and ideas of software risk management into the day-to-day working practices of the company.

1.5.1 Stages

In defining this risk management strategy there are some major stages that are performed (see Figure 1.5). These stages are:

1 Identify who will have accountability (roles and responsibilities)
2 Identify stakeholder groups (ownership)

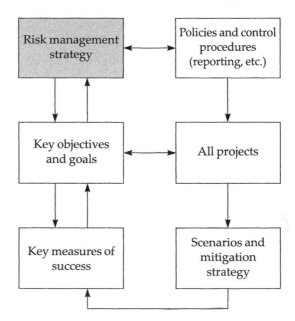

Figure 1.5
Risk management
strategy model

3 Identify the key objectives
4 Identify key measures of success
5 Identify key risks and issues
6 Prepare mitigation scenarios
7 Prepare a baseline plan
8 Establish control procedures.

1.5.1.1 Accountability (roles and responsibilities)

In the management and delivery of projects (software or otherwise) many people will have a part to play. People involved in risk management may have specific responsibilities as risk owners; or they may have a more general involvement as part of project management, procurement and management of operational services. The risk management strategy must acknowledge this diversity of input at the highest level.

All strategic initiatives require support from the top and there needs to be *clarity of who does what* and perhaps more to the point *whom is accountable*. For example, the project manager is likely to be the individual with day-to-day responsibility for implementing the mitigation strategy and monitoring its impact on the risk, and reporting on their effectiveness to the project board or risk owners. On the other hand, project directors are likely to be responsible for ensuring that risks have been properly identified and assessed across their particular areas. In addition they may have responsibility for raising awareness, knowledge and skills and to encourage participation in risk management. They will certainly be expected to review the risk management strategy with their project teams.

As means of an example, Figure 1.6 shows the tasks and responsibilities matrix of project manager and team members and timings of those actions in the risk management process.

Stages ⟶					
Identify	**Analyse**	**Plan**	**Track**	**Control**	**Review**
Who: Project manager	Who: Whole project team	Who: Project manager	Who: Project office	Who: Project office	Who: Project manager and other team members
When: Start of project	When: Start of project	When: Start of project	When: As required	When: As required	When: As required

Figure 1.6 Risk responsibility matrix

1.5.1.2 Stakeholder groups

Stakeholders are one of the most important groups to consult yet in projects stakeholders are numerous and are sometimes difficult to identify. One method for identifying stakeholder groups in the software community is the use of a 'contrast' or 'maximum' variation sampling procedure. This can be used to define local groupings around risks. Each individual interviewed is asked to identify another who will have the most different perceptions on the risk than his/her own. The process of interviewing and identifying new respondents with contrasting views is repeated until several main issues or themes emerge. These themes each represent a stakeholder group. This approach enables the identification of groups with conflicting or different values without asking direct questions that may be socially unacceptable to answer (McAllister 1999).

Another approach to stakeholder identification is to produce a stakeholder map. This is a simple process involving the following steps:

- Identify who's who in this project – key players, stakeholders, internal, external – and place them around the project
- Draw in reporting and communication lines
- Identify risks per stakeholder
- Mark anticipated conflict areas and relationships
- Draw in weak and strong connections.

Once you have drawn this map, it can be used to identify strategies to avert risks and enhance relationships and communication. The World Bank suggests some guiding questions for identifying stakeholders:

- Who might be affected (positively or negatively) by the risk to be addressed?
- Who are the 'voiceless' for whom special efforts may have to be made?
- Who are the representatives of those likely to be affected?
- Who is responsible for what is intended?
- Who is likely to mobilize for or against what is intended?
- Who can make what is intended more effective through their participation or less effective by their non-participation or outright opposition?
- Who can contribute financial and technical resources?
- Whose behaviour has to change for the effort to succeed?

(McManus 2002)

When assessing the risk or importance of stakeholders to a project's success, the use of 'checklist' questions is a good way of structuring thoughts and obtaining answers to which policy or strategy may be developed. For example:

- Which risks, affecting which stakeholders, does the project seek to address or alleviate?
- For which stakeholders does the project place a priority on meeting their needs, interests and expectations?
- Which stakeholder interests converge most closely with policy and project objectives?

1.5.1.3 Key objectives

Refer to earlier discussion point 1.4.

1.5.1.4 Key measures of success

Given the complexity of software projects identifying key measures of success is perhaps easier said than done. As previously stated there is a correlation between objectives and goals. At a micro level it is convenient to align these measures with our political, economic, business, and technical risk classification.

It is prudent to involve and derive measures from the stakeholders as assumptions are often misleading. It is important to find what the senior managers want and state this in terms they can understand so that risk can be identified easily and risks also will not be overlooked. In some cases the senior managers may not know what it is that they exactly want, so helping them derive a success measure ensures that when the project is finished the manager can be shown that the stated objectives have been met and the project is aligned with stakeholder needs. See example in Figure 1.4.

1.5.1.5 Key risks and issues

Regardless of size and scope, every project is threatened by risk. Software projects are especially susceptible to risk due to the speed of development in the field and its rapidly changing environment. In 1991 Barry Boehm identified a 'Top-10' list of major software development areas that threatened the success of projects and where risk must be addressed:

1 Skill shortfalls
2 Unrealistic schedules and budgets
3 Stability of external or off-the-shelf software
4 Requirements mismatch
5 User interface mismatch
6 Architecture, performance, quality
7 Requirement changes
8 Legacy software
9 Externally performed tasks
10 Straining computer science capabilities.

(Boehm 1991)

A more recent audit (2001) on a number of large, medium and small software projects identified a number of key risk areas. These have been ordered 11–20 in relation to their probability of occurrence and severity (or impact) to the project. These conclusions, based on risk assessments performed on 42 software projects undertaken between 1994 and 2000, include:

11 Stability of development infrastructure
12 Infrastructure limitations

13 Procurement of infrastructure
14 Multi-site software development
15 Untested development methodologies
16 Regulatory standards (for example, health and safety)
17 Inadequate test strategy
18 Development team involved in multiple projects or other activities
19 Communication problems
20 Availability of test sites or personnel.

(McManus 2001)

Robert Charette explains there are subtle environmental factors often overlooked when identifying sources of risk in software projects. They include:

- Software developments are very complex. The software problem has numerous elements with extremely complicated interrelationships.
- Problem element relationships can be multidimensional. The laws of proportionality do not govern changes in elements. It is well documented that adding more people to a project that is behind schedule, in many instances, will make it even later.
- Software problem elements are unstable and changeable. Although cost and schedule may be fixed, actual costs in labour and time to complete are difficult to project.
- The development process is dynamic. Conditions ceaselessly change; thus, project equilibrium is seldom achieved. The environment is never static – hardware malfunctions, personnel quit, and contractors do not deliver.
- People are an essential software development element and a major source of risk. Economic or technical problems are easy to deal with. The higher level complications, multidimensional ambiguities, and changing environment caused by conflicting human requirements, interaction, and desires are what cause problems. Software development is full of problems because it is a very human endeavour.

(Charette 1989)

Additionally, there are other interrelated factors that contribute to software risk. These factors are:

- Communication about risk is one of the most difficult, yet important, practices you must establish in your project.

Naturally people do not want to talk about potential problems. Rather than confronting imaginary problems whilst they are still in the risk stage, they wind up having to deal with them after they become full-blown, real problems. Then there is a lot of communication! Effective risk planning only occurs when people are willing to talk about risks in a non-threatening, constructive environment.

- Software size can affect the accuracy and efficacy of estimates. Interdependence amongst software elements increases exponentially as size increases. With extremely large software systems, handling complexity through decomposition becomes increasingly difficult because even decomposed elements may be unmanageable.
- Software architecture also affects software risk. Architectural structure is the ease with which functions can be modularized and the hierarchical nature of information to be processed. It is also development team structure, its relationship with the user and to one another, and the ease with which the human structure can develop the software architecture.

(Pressman 1993)

1.5.1.6 Mitigation scenarios

Risk mitigation encompasses prevention, control and management. Structured effectively, a risk mitigation programme will prevent risk and reduce the cost of losses. One approach to risk mitigation involves the developing of scenarios, see Figure 1.7.

Risk scenarios provide a framework for analysing and eliminating the unknowns within software projects. The basic approach is summarized below:

- Agree the boundary of the project
- Prepare initial scenarios
- Analyse scenarios
- Map problems and issues
- Identify key risk areas (use 80:20 rule)
- Prepare mitigation strategy and publish.

The outputs from these scenarios can be used throughout the project as go/no-go decision points. For example, the no-go decision can be made if the project reaches a point where it cannot mitigate a risk, or determines that the cost of mitigating a risk exceeds the value of the project. In such circumstances further analysis should be undertaken to ensure the benefit of

> **Scenario No. 1**
>
> **Parallel development efforts increase project complexity**
>
> Each development effort performed in support of the project transition represents a full system life cycle project. These multiple, concurrent efforts add to the management complexity of project implementation by requiring planning and concurrent monitoring of differing technical efforts, interdependent schedules, staffing issues, etc. With the increase of variables that must be considered at any one time, the potential is increased for a problem with a specific effort to be missed or for multiple efforts to fall behind schedule before corrective action can be taken.
>
> **Risk and impact**
>
> 1 Technical (moderate)
> 2 Schedule (high)
> 3 Cost (high).
>
> **Mitigation strategies**
>
> - Require that development plans for each project implementation integrate tightly with the project master transition schedule.
> - Limit the number of implementation projects in progress at any given time to a manageable number (determined based on the complexity of each project, available staff, duration, and nature of efforts to be performed in parallel).
> - Ensure that the project transition organization has the authority to act as a strong, central management and co-ordination function, and that each implementation project is responsible to the transition organization for the successful integration of the project into the overall project transition.
> - Obtaining qualified programme management staff and integration support necessary to hold effort together. Ensure that these staff are in place prior to commencing transition activities; once work is underway, the difficulty of trying to catch up with or undo past mistakes will overwhelm attempts to keep up with or prevent day-to-day issues.

Figure 1.7
Example of risk
mitigation scenario

mitigation outweighs the risk to the project and organization. Take, for example, the advice of Roger Rainbow reported in *The Economist*:

> *Scenario writing is not primarily about forecasting the future. It is designed to help in the construction and testing of specific strategies, which it can do in three ways. First, by educating decision makers about uncertainty and helping them to understand and challenge their own presumptions. Second, scenarios can be used in a formal way as a starting point for strategy development. Third, a conscious use of scenarios helps managers to adjust course in the light of events.*

(Rainbow 2001)

1.5.1.7 Baseline plan

Once all the risks are understood, the project manager can put in place baseline plans that will either transfer, eliminate, reduce or ignore the risk. Accountability for the necessary actions needs to be assigned at this stage. This will be discussed further in Chapters 2–3.

These baseline plans need to be reviewed and updated. This review process facilitates up-to-date reporting to all levels of the organization and clear visibility as to the status of the risks within the project. See also point 1.6.1.3.

1.5.1.8 Control procedures

Finally, an important function in the cycle is keeping track of those risks which pose the highest threat. As discussed tracking involves identification of your project's highest-risk issues and tracking progress towards resolving those issues through subsequent progress reports. The major risk management benefits are similar to those of cost/schedule/performance tracking plus the added ones of identifying and maintaining a high level risk consciousness. Tracking becomes critical because the one risk attribute whose influence is difficult to predict is 'time'. Generalizations about risk made early in the project can (and often do) decay with time. One reason for performing risk tracking is to keep a predictable, unpredictable, or unknown risk from becoming a known one. See also point 1.6.1.4.

1.6 Risk management paradigm

One question frequently asked by project managers is: How do I make trade-offs among the risk factors affecting software quality, cost overrun, and time delay in project completion? In risk management the project manager often attempts to answer three questions:

1 What can go wrong?
2 What is the likelihood that it would go wrong?
3 What are the consequences?

Answers to these questions help project managers to identify, measure and evaluate the consequences and impacts on risk. The remaining risk analysis builds on the risk assessment process by seeking answers to a second set of questions:

1 What can be done?
2 What options are available?
3 What are their associated trade-offs in terms of cost, benefits, and risk?
4 What are the impacts of current management decisions on future options?

Only when these questions are addressed in the broader context of management can risk management be realized. This is the domain of the risk management paradigm (Haimes 1991).

1.6.1 Risk paradigm

The risk paradigm exceeds all risk analysis activities discussed earlier. For this reason, it constitutes the foundation of each stage in the model depicted in Figure 1.5.

The risk management paradigm (Figure 1.8) depicts the different activities involved in the management of risk associated with software development. The paradigm is represented by a circle to emphasize that risk management is a continuous process, while the arrows show the logical flow of information between activities. Communication is placed in the centre of the paradigm because it is both the conduit through which all information flows and, often, the largest obstacle in risk management – see also Figure 1.1. Essentially, the paradigm is a framework for software risk management. From this

Figure 1.8
Risk management paradigm (copyright Software Engineering Institute, Carnegie Mellon University, Pittsburgh, Pennsylvania)

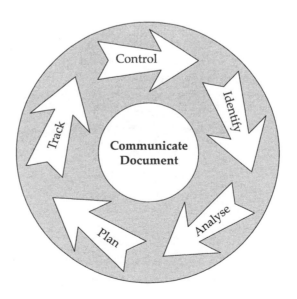

framework, a project may structure a risk management practice best fitting into its project management structure.

A brief description of each risk management paradigm activity is summarized below.

1.6.1.1 Identify

The purpose of identification is to consider risks before they become problems and to incorporate this information into the project management process. Anyone in a project can identify risks to the project. Each individual has particular knowledge about various parts of a project. During Identify, uncertainties and issues about the project are transformed into distinct (tangible) risks that can be described and measured.

1.6.1.2 Analyse

The purpose of analysis is the conversion of risk data into risk decision-making information. Analysis provides the project manager with the basis to work on the most appropriate risks.

1.6.1.3 Plan

Planning is the function of deciding what, if anything, should be done about a risk or set of related risks. In this function, decisions and mitigation strategies are developed based on current knowledge of project risks. The plan for a specific risk can take many forms. For example:

- Mitigate the impact of risk by developing a contingency plan (together with a trigger event) should the risk occur.
- Avoid a risk by changing the product design or the development process.
- Accept the risk and take no further action, thus accepting the consequences if the risk occurs.
- Study the risk further to acquire more information and better determine its characteristics to enable wiser decision making.

The key to risk planning is to consider the future consequences of a decision made today (Higuera and Haimes 1996).

1.6.1.4 Track

Tracking is the process by which risk status data are acquired, compiled, and reported. The purpose of tracking is to collect accurate, timely, and relevant risk information and to present it in a clear and easily understood manner to the appropriate people/group. Tracking is done by those responsible for monitoring watched or mitigated risks. Tracking status information becomes critical to performing the control function. Supporting information, such as schedule and budget variances, critical path changes, and project/performance indicators can be used as triggers, thresholds, and risk- or plan-specific measures where appropriate.

1.6.1.5 Control

The purpose of the control function is to make informed, timely, and effective decisions regarding risks and their mitigation plans. It is the process that takes in tracking status information and decides exactly what to do based on the reported data. Controlling risks involves analysing the status reports, deciding how to proceed, and then implementing those decisions.

1.6.1.6 Communicate

The SEI model (Figure 1.8) places communication at the centre for good reason – without effective communication, no risk management approach can be viable. While communication facilitates interaction amongst the elements of the model, there are higher level communications to consider as well. In order to be analysed and managed correctly, risks must be communicated to and between the appropriate organization levels. This includes levels within the development project and organization, within the customer organization and most especially, across that threshold between the developer, the customer, and, where different, the user. (I will discuss these points in more detail later.)

1.7 Developing the organization for software risk management

It was stated in point 1.4.2 that organizations of low capability experience the highest incidence of failure. Developing the organization's capability to manage risk is a prerequisite and benefits customers and providers alike. As a starting point you should consider an organizational approach and structure that is consistent with the size of your organization, the complexity of its operations, the maturity of the risk management process and the fit with other planning systems already in use. Generally, an

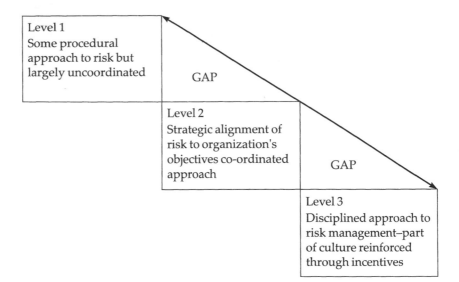

Figure 1.9
Three levels of risk
maturity

organization should start with the simpler structures and move to the more complex arrangements, see Figure 1.9.

Good structures and processes, along with a sense of readiness in the organization are all-important components of the organization's readiness, but it is the people who will actually implement the risk management approach adopted by the organization.

What support will be needed to make sure that people in the organization are able to implement risk management? Do not overlook the importance of people.

The long-term success of any risk management programme is contingent upon the people in the organization being placed in a strong position to develop a positive attitude to risk management.

1.7.1 Cultural considerations

It is important to develop a risk management culture within the organization. This can be achieved through communication and dialogue, for example briefing sessions, training and education as well as briefing papers. The establishment of incentives or rewards for successfully applying the principles of risk management may also lead to a risk management mindset being developed across an organization.

Use lessons from the past to highlight the importance of risk management. Lessons could draw on past failures that demonstrate when analysed how the use of good risk management techniques could have prevented such failures or at least minimized the effect of the failure. Explaining the loss in value terms, or in terms of the long-term effect on staff, could dramatize why it is important always to consider the risks when approaching a business problem or initiating a software project.

A review of the literature identifies a number of common points that can be distilled into an eight-point plan for ensuring a paradigm shift in the organization occurs. These eight points are:

1 Acceptance of a risk management framework
2 Commitment from executives/the board
3 Establish the risk response strategy
4 Monitoring of risk management process
5 Assigning responsibility for risk management change process
6 Reinforce risk culture through human resource mechanisms
7 Communications and training
8 Commitment to resourcing.

By following this plan and applying the principles of continual improvement, a risk management culture in the organization should develop.

I will conclude this chapter by looking at an area of software project management that is influencing many organizations to revisit their strategies and policies on risk management – the excessive use and adoption of litigation here in the UK and in the USA.

1.8 Risk management and litigation

The costs of failed software projects or IT services can be substantial, including lost sales, legal fees, litigation costs, system failure costs, lost management time, lost employee time, incidental expenses, vendor charges for phone support, and damages to the business. When failure occurs, one of the first remedies is instigating litigation against the vendor or service provider. Unfortunately, using the law as a remedy is widely misunderstood. For example, people often insist that IT vendors and software developers cannot be sued with ease. This is absolutely untrue. Depending on what you're willing to count as a 'computer malpractice' case, the number of computer related lawsuits in the USA, for example, is high. It is not unusual for a large software development organization to have over 50 active cases on its hands. Software warranties have done little to reduce this flood of litigation – see, for example, the work undertaken by Gonulkiewicz (1997).

IT organizations are experiencing an epidemic of litigation related to software projects. Take the following story as an example.

In 1998 a subsidiary of Johnson & Johnson was accused of failing to notify the US Food and Drug Administration of a *software mistake in a diabetes diagnostic programme*. This eventually led to a plea of guilty to three misdemeanour charges in Federal Court and the payment of a $60 million fine in late 2000. How did Johnson & Johnson respond initially? Its chief executive, Ralph S. Larsen, was quoted as saying: 'Mistakes were made in the Lifescan situation. There were errors in judgement. We did too little too late.' (*The New York Times*, 15 January, 2001). Is that taking responsibility? I think not. It is a passive evasion implying that 'others' in the organization are responsible. What Mr Larsen should have said is: 'I take full responsibility, as chief executive of Johnson & Johnson, and I will make sure that this type of event does not happen again.' Would this have changed the financial penalty? Possibly not, but it would have started to rebuild confidence in Johnson & Johnson (Kloman 2001).

1.8.1 The litigants

There are two distinct groups who will most likely end up in litigation. These include those who purchase a product or suite of products to increase efficiency and productivity. Disputes amongst the first group of litigants are characterized by businesses with little experience in IT development. The second group of litigants is the IT vendor and IT purchasers. Both parties are sophisticated in terms of their understanding of the dynamics of the IT market and will usually have products or services, which purportedly complement each other.

Areas of common concern include:

- Contract law (includes breach of contract and warranties)
- Tort law (includes negligence and fraud)
- Copyright protection.

1.8.2 Litigation cases

A search of the recent literature on litigation cases points to software quality as one of the most important issues in software development projects. That is: What was the quality of the delivered software and was it fit for purpose? This question raises another question of just what is meant by 'software quality'? The ready answer from the experienced IT expert is that questions concerning 'software quality' essentially come down to: Does the delivered software meet its stated requirements? Thus the risk-legal litigation conflict common to all such software cases may be succinctly put as 'fitness for purpose versus statement of requirements'. However, this 'conflict' manifests itself in different ways, with a different emphasis, for different specific cases. This is certainly true in the case of tort law. Take the following case as an example.

An NCR salesman performed a detailed analysis of Chatlos' business operations and computer needs. He then advised Chatlos to buy NCR equipment. Relying on NCR's advice, Chatlos bought a system that did not provide many of the promised functions. Chatlos sued. NCR was held liable for breach of contract. The court discussed Chatlos' claim of malpractice:

> *The novel concept of a new tort called 'computer malpractice' is premised upon a theory of elevated responsibility on the part of those who render computer sales and service. Plaintiff equates the sale and servicing of computer systems with established theories of professional malpractice. Simply because an activity is technically complex and important to the business community does not mean that greater potential liability must attach. In the absence of sound precedential authority, the Court declines the invitation to create a new tort.*

This case and its refusal to recognize the validity of a lawsuit for defects in vendor systems design have been widely quoted (Federal Supplement 1979).

1.8.3 Risk v. litigation

Most of the litigation cases I have reviewed have involved organizations that failed to do any risk management at all. Risk and the propensity of litigation would reduce substantially and software quality would improve dramatically if developers paid more attention to just three areas:

- Documentation
- Testing
- Planning.

Under pressure to release products, most software is not properly tested before its release. Today's computer programs are huge and complex and it is harder to test software with millions of lines of code. Too often the testing falls to the unfortunate user who decides to use a new program or IT system. Is it any wonder that many astute computer users avoid the first release of a program, preferring to await the next version that fixes the initial release? It is a sad fact that litigation related to software projects and information systems will only continue to grow as we move in the twenty-first century, with increased software complexity, the use of networks and the rush to get new products and services to market.

1.9 Self-assessment checklist

Ask yourself	Yes	No	Not sure
Vision and objectives			
• Does the organization have a concise vision of risk management?	☐	☐	☐
• Is the vision shared within the organization?	☐	☐	☐
• Does the organization have a defined framework and plan for introducing risk management?	☐	☐	☐
• Does the organization have senior management support for the introduction of risk management?	☐	☐	☐
• Does the framework allow for different categories of risk to be managed independently or in an integrated fashion across the organization?	☐	☐	☐
• Does the organization have a policy on litigation?	☐	☐	☐
• Does the organization have the appropriate competencies to introduce risk management?	☐	☐	☐
• Does the organization know which stakeholder groups need influencing?	☐	☐	☐
• Does the organization have clear goals and objectives?	☐	☐	☐
• Are the objectives achievable?	☐	☐	☐
• Are the objectives measurable?	☐	☐	☐
Accountability			
• Does the organization have a clear view of who is responsible for risk management?	☐	☐	☐
• Does everyone know his or her role?	☐	☐	☐
• Does everyone have clearly defined terms of reference?	☐	☐	☐
• Is everyone committed to the goals of risk management?	☐	☐	☐
• Does the staff have sufficient knowledge and expertise in the domain of risk?	☐	☐	☐
Procedures			
• Does the organization have clearly defined, documented procedures to support the risk management framework?	☐	☐	☐
• Do all members of staff understand these procedures?	☐	☐	☐
• Does the organization have a procedure for reviewing its goals and objectives?	☐	☐	☐
• Does the organization have a procedure for reviewing its approach to risk management?	☐	☐	☐
• Does the organization have a procedure for reviewing its applied risk measures?	☐	☐	☐

Discovering risk in software development projects

2.1 Recap on Chapter 1

From the previous chapter you will have ascertained the importance of having a global perspective of risk. That is:

- Viewing software project risk within the context of the larger system definition, and
- Recognizing both the potential value of opportunity and the potential impact of adverse effects, such as cost, delay, and failure to meet project objectives.

It is also important to note that the software risk paradigm has three fundamentally different, albeit complementary objectives:

1 Risk prevention
2 Risk mitigation and correction
3 Protection from litigation (or financial loss).

In this chapter we will explore at a more detailed level some of the topics, issues and concerns highlighted in the previous chapter.

2.2 Identifying software risk

In software development projects the need to manage risk increases with the complexity of the project. Theorists (and some practitioners) agree there is an increasing need for more systematic methods and tools to supplement individual knowledge, judgement and experience. Human traits alone are often insufficient to address complex risk. There is some evidence to suggest that managers believe that they are managing risk in complex dimensions. In essence they are merely managing the basics, that is cost, scheduled delay and some isolated cases of technical risk.

Many of the most dramatic failures and issues in software projects are the result of risks that either remain unrecognized and/or ignored until they have already created serious consequences. The focus on risk is important because structured methods, even simple ones, can be effective in identifying risk.

2.2.1 Methods

The identification of risk (see point 1.6.1.1) will require the use of qualitative methods. Techniques such as brainstorming, SWOT analysis, and threat scenarios used together ensure complete coverage and the identification of the specific sources of risk. The end product of risk identification will be a list of risks, each of which is associated in some way with the accomplishment of organizational objectives (outputs) which are designed to accomplish the organizational goals in the time periods under study. These same techniques are used to address the project level risks within each of the four strategic areas. The main problem is to generate enough ideas so that all reasonable and significant risks are discovered. Any risk identification methods should have the following attributes:

1 They should examine all areas of the project in a systematic manner
2 They should be proactive rather than reactive
3 They should synthesize risk information from all available sources of risk information. Typical sources and uses are:

- Risk databases: a risk database is an ordered collection of information derived from experience on previous projects. A formal risk information system is a good way of ensuring that this information is captured for use on future projects.
- Risk checklists: a checklist is a list of areas where you might expect problems to occur. Checklists are specific to whatever type of project your organization undertakes, and must be developed specifically for your particular business or industry for more details.

- Information gathering techniques: is any technique which is not directed towards a specific, known area of risk, but is instead designed to elicit information from a wide range of individuals.
- Strengths, Weaknesses, Opportunities and Threats (SWOT) Analysis: SWOT analysis of a project usually examines it from the perspective of the parent organization of the project team. Normally this should be done before a commitment to take on the project is made. However, such an analysis can identify risks that are inherent in the organization's capabilities with regard to the project.
- Specialized techniques: under this category are included techniques that require specialized knowledge to perform usefully. These include techniques such as cause-and-effect diagrams and various forms of flowcharts.
- Lessons learned reports: sources of information from past projects used to identify key issues and provide guidance on best practice.

2.2.2 Qualitative methods and techniques

Successful practitioners in project management hardly ever perform quantitative analysis. Qualitative analysis of risk exposure is usually sufficient to sort through a large number of risks to select the most important. Quantitative analysis can be reserved for only those risks that require numerical justification or justification for mitigation and approval. I will now discuss those methods described below and noted in 1.3.2. They are:

- Brainstorming
- SWOT analysis
- Maps
- Checklists and questionnaires
- Peer interviews.

2.2.2.1 Brainstorming

Brainstorming is a simple but well-known and widely used problem-solving tool. With respect to risk the purpose of this technique is to identify as many risks as possible. There are just a few simple rules to follow:

1 No evaluating of any kind is allowed. Do not discuss any risk, just go on to the next one. When risks are judged, participants will feel the need to defend themselves and may not wish to

participate. Without full participation from all members, the creative process is hindered. Also, when members feel they are being judged, they will censor their ideas to conform to the group. We do not want conformity. We want the wild, spontaneous, and even the ridiculous. Wild and crazy risks can springboard more sensible ones or can be tamed later in the process. The goal at this stage is quantity and not quality.

2 Limit your discussion to one issue or risk type. Brainstorming needs a goal or something to focus on. It would be too confusing and distracting to try to solve all our problems at once. Look at risks that all members can speak on.

3 Build on what has been said and modify the ideas of others. This reduces the need for people to find the 'right' idea and helps keep the session more stimulating and fun.

The project manager should capture your ideas. He doesn't have to write down the ideas verbatim, but enough of the concept and key words to be able to remember the idea later. After the brainstorming session is over, the project manager will make good use of the participant's creativity. Before we rank or evaluate ideas, we will group them into related categories for review. This will make it easier to combine similar ideas on risk and weed out duplication. Decide which are possible and which can be eliminated; putting pluses and minuses by items is ideal.

Ranking the most promising ideas. Write all the possible ideas on newsprint or chalkboard. It is important every member can see what is being ranked. We may want to use a rating system such as 1 being lowest and 5 being highest. Select those with greatest potential and high ranking priority for either implementation or refinement by committee or the group. We may need to have participants do some further research on applicability before the group can pick a top idea to implement.

2.2.2.2 SWOT analysis

SWOT analysis is a simple, easy to understand method. It was originally developed as a tool in formulating strategies and policies. Project managers and their staff can use the method to analyse threats and resultant risk within a project (Figure 2.1). The process is a simple one – simply list what you believe to be the key strengths, weaknesses, opportunities and threats to a project, and concentrate your efforts on defining risk in relation to threats.

Potential opportunities	Potential threats
1. New hardware technology	1. Performance issues
2. New methods of analysis	2. Competency issues
3. New development tools	3. Learning curves/productivity
4. New testing tools	4. Performance issues

The individual project manager working with a small group of people best performs SWOT. Group participation is particularly effective in providing structure, objectivity, clarity and focus to discussions about risk which might otherwise tend to wander or else be strongly influenced by politics and personalities.

In order to be most effectively used, a SWOT analysis needs to be flexible. Software development project situations change with the passage of time and an updated analysis should be made frequently. SWOT is neither cumbersome nor time consuming and is effective because of its simplicity. Used creatively, SWOT can form a foundation upon which to construct numerous risk analyses.

2.2.2.3 Maps

A map is a good method to decide what issues affect other issues. Maps show all of the factors involved in a process and how these factors are interrelated. By focusing on relationships between issues, the map can unveil significant aspects that might otherwise be overlooked.

A map depicts influences and processes as groups of circles, arrows, squares, etc. These maps can take on many different forms, depending on the relationships you want to depict. Maps can be highly stylized – spatial accuracy is not required for this overview.

Maps can be laid on an actual map to show how risks affect each other or can take the form of an influence map. Steps:

- List the steps in the process or links in the relationship that you want to depict.
- Create a key to show whether something is a cause, result, issue, decision point, or other pertinent factor.
- Either superimpose these steps or links onto an existing map of the area, draw a stylized map that highlights these steps or links, or create a flowchart that shows a process.

- Clearly label these steps or links.
- Draw influence arrows between these steps or links. (Different types of influences may require different types of arrows.)

You may want to highlight a central decision, by placing this main parameter in the middle of the page. Relationships should be kept as simple as possible. For reciprocal relationships, depict only the stronger influence. Use one map for each main risk. Use the same symbols throughout a document or study to avoid confusing the reader. See Figure 2.2.

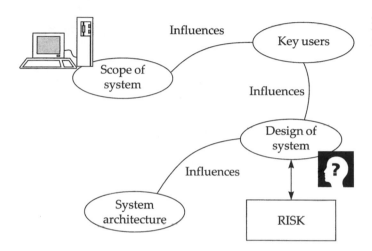

Figure 2.2
Example of a map

2.2.2.4 Checklists and questionnaires

Checklists and questionnaires are useful tools to obtain information on potential risks – certainly if used at the start of the requirements phase. Assessment checklists are good for identifying what can go wrong, and the likely consequences of it going wrong. Questionnaires take longer to construct and require more effort to analyse but again it is a very useful method of gathering information on potential areas of risk. Some global IT service providers use questionnaires at the bidding phase – to identify the risk of bidding or perhaps more important to qualify out.

2.2.2.5 Peer interviews

The use of interviews to extracting risks is considered by many practitioners to be an effective and practical way of gaining valuable input to the risk process. The method broadly consists of a series of interview sessions, each interview group consisting only of peers, for example project managers, analysts, database designers, etc. Like the brainstorming approach the method requires rules that define the composition of peer groups. These are:

- No reporting relationships amongst attendees within one group
- Vertical coverage (that is representation across the organizational hierarchy)
- Horizontal coverage (that is all functional groups relevant to the project).

For several reasons (*group dynamics, follow-up probing, observing and reacting to non-verbal responses, etc.*) groups should be limited to at most five participants. In general, five interview sessions are necessary. A typical project and interview schedule will involve individual sessions for each of the following four groupings: technical architects, software developers, domain experts, and project management.

Each evaluation team member is asked to record his perception of uncertainties expressed in the interview subjects' responses. The collective team members' notes represent the raw risk data as extracted from the project staff. The interview protocol is such that the uncovering of uncertainties and issues is facilitated on the basis of the discussion rather than on a strict partitioning of the interview session. Team members are encouraged to interject with context-sensitive probing questions and to follow up on any discussion that seems to point to a risk issue. As is the case in any evaluative situation, evasive behaviour on the part of an interviewee works counter to interview success. To offset the evasive tendency the participants should be assured that no information surfaced will be attributed either to any one individual or to any one group. A technique used by the evaluation team to overcome evasive behaviour is to request follow-up, tangible evidence to support questionable assertions made during the interview.

Checklists are often used during each interview session to seed the conversation and to elicit sources of uncertainty that may put the successful completion of the project at risk.

2.3 Most common software project risks

Designing, developing and implementing software projects is a complex undertaking, involving highly uncertain activities.

Technology is used in increasingly advanced ways involving networks, advanced communications and widespread access to all types of information. Problems can (and do) occur at every stage of the life cycle: planning, requirement analysis, design (logical and physical) build, test, and implementation.

As previously stated research indicates that there is a relationship between those problems which lead to failure and those characteristics of the project. Such characteristics include size, complexity, timeframe, technological innovation, uncertainty, governance and management. Software development projects are designed and implemented by large multidisciplinary project teams, who are responsible for producing complex systems involving highly interactive hardware and software. Frequently project requirements may change during project development to take account of both emerging technologies and new techniques. Given the multiplicity and variety of interfaces which exist between the various phases, across the numerous disciplines and along the different levels of management audience, it is not surprising that many projects fail to be completed or deliver the expected benefits. A framework developed by Cash, McFarlan and McKenney (1992) identifies three important groups of factors that relate to the inherent implementation of risk. These are those factors relating to:

1 The project size such as staffing, levels duration, cost, and number of departments affected
2 The technology such as level of technical expertise, emergent technology to be used, technical difficulty of design and experience of similar projects
3 The project structures such as clear requirements, fixed and certain outcomes, and the absence of changes in specification during the lifetime of the project.

(Cash, McFarlan and McKenney 1992)

Work undertaken by Corder on risk classification categorized the relative magnitude of risk for a number of factors associated with software project risk. Corder stated that project size, project definition, user commitment and stability, project time and the number of system interfaces are all high risk factors whilst the number of geographic sites, functional newness and number of project phases are all low risk factors. Factors such as functional complexity, number of user departments, newness of technology/vendor and user experience of technology are classified as medium risk.

A pioneer of software development projects, Barry Boehm developed a risk driven approach to software development in his spiral model, wherein areas of uncertainty that can result in project risk are identified at an early stage. Depending on the kind of risks involved, the spiral model uses one or a mix of existing approaches, such as prototyping, simulation, benchmarking, or analytical modelling. Once the risks are evaluated the relative remaining risks are assessed and these determine further development actions. This approach relies heavily on the ability of software developers to manage sources of project risk. Experienced project managers will thereby be able to assess project risks more readily and accurately (Balint and Nottingham 1995).

2.3.1 Classification of risks

Using the techniques described in 2.2.2, one simple method of classifying common risks is to follow the software development life cycle (SDLC). Risks can be identified as belonging to the various stages of the SDLC, namely: planning requirement analysis, design (logical and physical) build, test, and implementation (that is, the installation of the hardware, software, user training and ongoing support). See Figure 2.3.

2.3.1.1 Key discussion points

Although not exhaustive by any means the list in Figure 2.3 does provide a reasonable starting point for examining risk in software projects. It is clear that software project teams can produce reasonable quality software systems without any structured approach to risk (but at what cost?), evidence would suggest that the odds are against you in the long term. Take, for example, the following case: systems development staff found that time constraint for projects actively prevented a formal approach to undertaking software enhancements. There was insufficient time allowed to produce or revise documentation (that is data models, diagrams, etc.). Development personnel often tried to minimize their workload to meet deadlines. Reducing the number of steps taken to do the task and reducing the amount of documentation were two ways to achieve this. In other words they took short cuts which finally resulted in the project being undermined and the client refusing to sign off the work.

Stage 1: Planning/mobilization
Common software risks:
- Ineffective resource management
- Inaccurate estimates
- Inadequate planning
- Inadequate skills
- Inadequate communication
- Inappropriate deliverables
- Inadequate contract management
- Inadequate stakeholder involvement
- Inappropriate locations
- Infighting between managers

Stage 2: Requirements analysis
Common software risks:
- Ignorance of formalized methodologies
- Inappropriate case tools
- Inadequate skills
- Inappropriate team size
- Lack of knowledge of business processes
- Lack of user involvement
- Lack of clearly defined user requirements
- Lack of non-functional requirements
- Misleading information from the user

Stage 3: Design
Common software risks:
- Inappropriate architecture
- Inappropriate tools
- Poor logical design
- Poor physical design
- Poor interface design
- Lack of vision
- Lack of user sign-off
- Scope creep

Stage 4: Build
Common software risks:
- Inappropriate development languages
- Inappropriate standards and documentation
- Lack of knowledge of tool set
- Reliance on one tool set
- Poor release management
- Poor configuration management
- Poor build specifications

Stage 5: Test
Common software risks:
- Inappropriate acceptance criteria
- Inappropriate testing tools
- Inappropriate test methodology
- Inappropriate starting point
- No authority to overcome impediments
- Lack of involvement in UAT
- Lack of internal support
- Lack of testing interface
- Lack of equipment
- Lack of stress loading
- Overreliance on beta testing
- Overreliance on testers who are domain experts
- Poor-quality software

Stage 6: Implementation
Common software risks:
- Poor communication
- Lack of planning
- Lack of implementation strategy
- Lack of personnel to see through implementation
- Lack of user training
- Lack of time for installation
- Incomplete handoffs between groups
- Poor user documentation
- Poor technical documentation
- Poor communication between groups (especially third party suppliers)
- Poor on-site testing
- Poor post-implementation support

Figure 2.3 Some common risks within the SDLC

Point 2
The importance of communication between groups in a software project should not be underestimated. The lack of communication can be a major source of risk (certainly in projects with more than ten people). In some projects, for example, a different

41

person from the one who designs the system undertakes the analysis of requirements. Unless the information is communicated between project participants, errors and omissions can easily be introduced through communication problems between the staff concerned. The project manager should attempt to overcome such communication problems by ensuring that requirements are the prime means of communication between all concerned on the project.

Point 3

One risk identified time and again in software projects is the testing of systems. In projects the testing of systems is still based on the code rather than the original requirements or software design specifications. System testing advocates the production of test plans early in the SDLC, usually around the design stage, to ensure that the organizational requirements are tested. This helps to reduce quality problems. Testing the system in an artificial environment rather than one that matched the operational circumstances is another source of risk. In particular with large data networks performance problems are encountered when the system is implemented. This is because the test environment does not realistically emulate the data and transaction volumes that are likely to be encountered in the project environment.

2.4 Risk taxonomy

In 2.2 we briefly discussed the use of questionnaires as a means of identifying potential areas of project risk. One such risk questionnaire used in the development of software projects and developed by the Software Engineering Institute is the Taxonomy-Based Risk Questionnaire. The questionnaire is structured into three main classes of software risk. Namely:

1 Product engineering
2 Development environment
3 Programme constraints.

Each of these categories is subdivided further (see Figure 2.4), narrowing the focus on particular aspects of risk. The questionnaire can be used in a practical, efficient manner consistent with the objective of surfacing project risks. The questionnaire was developed using extensive expertise and multiple field tests.

Almost all the questions below were taken from the product engineering section (that is the technical aspects of the work to be accomplished) although some have been added to cater for the uniqueness of project management.

2.4.1 Requirements

Stability/Completeness (assessed by evaluating the amount of information in the requirements):

- Are the requirements changing or yet to be determined? Consider the risk if requirements are being added, changed or are undetermined.
- Does the instructor have unwritten requirements/expectations? Consider the risk if some project requirements were given to you verbally.

Clarity (assessed by evaluating your comprehension of the requirements):

- Are you able to understand the requirements as written? Consider the risk if key requirements are vaguely stated (ambiguous).

Feasibility (assessed by evaluating the possible difficulties that might arise later in the project):

- Are there any requirements that are technically difficult to implement? Consider the risk if you aren't sure how a requirement could be implemented in the development language.

Tracking (assessed by evaluating the ability to keep requirements visible during the project):

- Do you have a plan to track the requirements throughout the design, coding and testing phases? Consider the risk if requirements *fall out* of the process and are not handled in the correct phase.

2.4.2 Design

Functionality (assessed by evaluating the feature set and capabilities of the product):

- Are there any specified algorithms that may not (or only partially) satisfy the requirements? Consider the risk that the algorithms may be wrong, incomplete, or too complex.

Difficulty (assessed by evaluating the effort involved in producing the design):

- Does any of the design depend on unrealistic or optimistic assumptions? Consider the risk if requirements were too optimistic regarding design.
- Are there any requirements or functions that are difficult to design? Consider, for example, the risk that a complex tree search may require more effort to design.

Interfaces (assessed by evaluating the connections between components, or to the outside world):

- Are the internal and external interfaces well defined? Consider the risk of complex or numerous connections between components or systems.

Performance and quality (assessed by evaluating the functionality and quality of the product):

- Are there any problems with the expected performance, or quality, of the design? Consider the risk of inadequate response or turnaround time, or lack of functionality.

Testability (assessed by evaluating the effort required to sufficiently test the product):

- Is the software going to be easy to test? Consider the risks of high complexity and what that may do in testing the product.

Hardware constraints (assessed by evaluating the hardware of the target or development platform):

- Does the development or target hardware limit your ability to meet any requirements? Consider the risk of limitations on hardware speed, size, availability and functionality.

Software reuse (assessed by evaluating the extent to which software is reused in the product):

- Does reused or re-engineered software exist? More problems than designing original software.

2.4.3 Code and unit test

Feasibility (assessed by evaluating the relative ease necessary to perform code and test):

- Are any parts of the product implementation not completely defined by the design specification? Consider the risk of not being able to track the requirements to the design, and then to the code.
- Are the selected algorithms and designs easy to implement? Consider the risk of overly complex components, or components with poor internal interfaces.

Testing:

- Is there sufficient time to perform the entire unit testing that you specified? Consider the risk of not having enough time in the schedule for this activity.
- Will compromises be made regarding unit testing if there are schedule problems? Consider who will compromise, and on what components. Consider what may be missed.

Coding/Implementation:

- Are the design specifications in sufficient detail to write the code? Consider the risk if the design is too high level.
- Is the design changing while coding is being done? Consider the scope of the changes; large changes could cause wasted coding effort.
- Is the language suitable for producing the software of this program? Consider the risk of using a relational language to crunch numbers (extreme case).
- Does your team have enough experience with the development language, platform or tools? Consider the risk if your team is not well represented in these areas.
- Is there a risk that a key component or module will not be complete or on schedule? Consider the risk, for example, that a parsing component is incomplete in the late coding phase.
- Are you comfortable with your team's estimate on coding time and effort? Consider the risk if you grossly underestimated the effort required of you.
- Do you have a plan for configuration management of the code? Consider the risk if there is no revision control or there is uncontrolled code modification.

2.4.4 Integration and test

Environment (assessed by evaluating the hardware and software support facilities and test cases):

- Will there be sufficient hardware to do adequate integration and testing?
- Is there any problem with developing realistic scenarios and test data to demonstrate any requirements? Consider the risk of meeting the schedule, and testing coverage.

Product (assessed by evaluating the integration and testing of groups of components):

- Have acceptance criteria been agreed to for all requirements? Consider the risk of not knowing exactly what is expected.
- Has sufficient product integration been specified, and has adequate time been allocated for it? Consider the risk of meeting the schedule and getting sufficient testing coverage.

System (assessed by evaluating the integration between the product and target hardware):

- Has sufficient system integration and system integration time been specified? Consider the risk of meeting the schedule and getting sufficient testing coverage.

Maintainability (assessed by evaluating the effort required to locate and fix errors):

- Is the product design and documentation adequate for another class to maintain the code? Consider the risk if this is a requirement.

Specifications:

- Are the test specifications adequate to fully test the system? Consider the risk of poorly written requirements or specifications.

2.4.5 Communication, team compatibility and motivation

Communication (assessed by evaluating the ability of the team to exchange information):

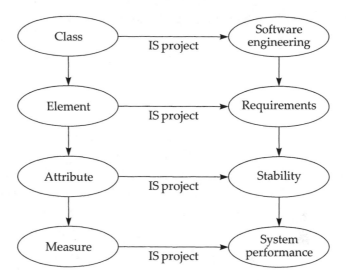

Figure 2.4
Software risk taxonomy
(McManus 2001)

- Is there a lack of good communication amongst your team?
- Is there a lack of good communication with your instructor about the project? Consider the risk to the quality of your work if you have incomplete information.

Compatibility of team (assessed by evaluating the ability of the team to work productively):

- Is your team familiar to you; have you worked together on a team project before? Consider the risk if the team is not comfortable working together, or has not done so before.
- Are tasks delegated in a fair manner amongst your team? Consider the risk if your team is not in agreement.

Motivation of team (assessed by evaluating the goals of the team):

- Is your team motivated to create a good product? Consider the risk to the project, if grades are the sole motivation.

(Pressman 1992; Carr *et al.* 1993;
Taxonomy-Based Risk Identification Questionnaire)

2.5 Risk mapping

As discussed in 2.3.1 part of the process of identification is to classify risks under some generic structure such as the software development life cycle. The ultimate purpose of classification is to understand the nature of the risks facing the project and to group any related risks so as to build cost-efficient mitigation plans. A holistic description of project risk situation can only be arrived at through a detailed analysis of the relations between all risk situations. Risk mapping makes it possible to determine the way in which various risks behave in relation to one another. The purpose of this highly extensive process is to identify possible diversification effects within a project's individual risk position. The product of this subprocess is a risk map (picture) which reveals the interdependent relationships between all the risks of an organization and forms the basis for structuring an all-encompassing integrated risk management solution.

Another reason for undertaking the risk mapping process is to exploit all possible different effects (related to the cost of risk) within an organization's overall risk situation – this is certainly the case with programme management. On cost grounds it may be considered expedient to group together certain types of risks into risk packages and appoint a risk manager to own the package (a point I will discuss later in this chapter).

2.5.1 Usefulness

The immediate usefulness of the risk mapping method lies in its ease of graphic representation and thus of communication to, and comprehension by, stakeholders and other senior decision makers. When coupled with other techniques, this method can usefully represent risks and when updated period-ically, it can capture periodicity in subjects' experience of risk. By distinguishing between the incidence of subjective risk perceptions, this method enhances understanding of the nature and variation of risk. This method can be quite helpful in the targeting of both research and support of interventions, in that it facilitates identification of the worries of specific software development programmes, or principal economic and project activity.

2.5.2 Tools and packages

The production of risk maps can be a time-consuming process – this is certainly true for large software projects or where there is wide diversification. Putting the map together is more easily accomplished if a tool is used. You will not be surprised to learn that there are hundreds of risk related software packages from which to select. Whilst I do not intend to discuss which are best, etc. I will, however, point out some of the key attributes in selecting such a tool. (See also Chapter 4, point 4.4.)

Like all software packages the key to success in which tool to select is establishing what your requirements (or needs) are. Of course functionality will be number one on any project manager's checklist of requirements. However, an organization purchasing a package must not only determine its functional requirements, but it must analyse available alternatives and compare and weight the functional characteristics of each product to the requirements. In this process similar requirements can be grouped into the general classifications listed below. These are:

- Product capabilities: functional requirements for the type of risk management software required, for example, be it operating system or application software.
- Technical support: including product documentation and system operating terms supported.
- Implementation: including report set-up, hardware requirements, software prerequisites, implementation effort, and complexity to change and training.
- Other aspects: including pricing, discounts, maintenance, the installed base of users, vendor information, and user group information.

In addition those purchasing risk software packages must realize that choosing a package involves many compromises (or trade-offs). Some required functions might be only partially met, whilst others will be missing entirely. In my experience purchasers of software do not always understand their own requirements, so they tend to select software based on specifications prepared by suppliers – this, of course, can be a dangerous action to adopt.

2.6 Risk statements

During the identification stage we will record a number of uncertainties and issues that will need to transcribe into clear and tangible risks that can be described and measured. One method of transcribing risk is by producing a risk statement, normally written as a single declaration concisely specifying the cause as well as its impact. See Figure 2.5.

The objective for a risk statement is that it is clear, concise (that is they should avoid the use of abbreviations, acronyms and

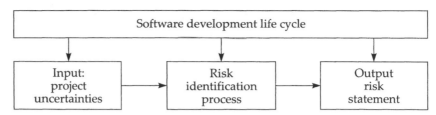

Figure 2.5
Risk statement input v.
output

irrelevant details) and sufficiently informative that the risk is easily understood (that is by managers and users alike). See Figure 2.7.

Risk statements should be produced in a standard format and should contain the *condition* and *consequence*. This format provides a complete picture of the risk, which is critical during the mitigation process. This statement of risk should become a baseline for all future actions.

The condition component focuses on what is currently causing concern; it must be something that is considered to be true or widely true. This component will provide information that is useful when determining how to address the issue of mitigation.

The consequence component focuses on the intermediate and the long-term impact of the risk. Understanding the depth and breadth of the impact is useful in determining how much time, resources, and effort should be allocated to the mitigation effort. Generally speaking a risk statement should have only one condition but may have more than one consequence, Figure 2.6.

In preparing the risk statement it is usually prudent to add additional information by way of a context box. The purpose of this context box is to ensure the original intent is captured. An effective context captures the essence of the risk by describing

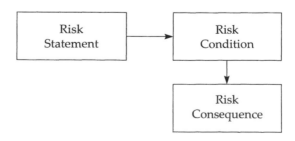

Figure 2.6
Risk condition

50

Project name: Description of project: Project phase: Risk reference no:	
Risk statement:	
Condition Given the condition (specify what the condition is)	Consequence There is a possibility that consequence will occur (specify the consequence)
Project manager:	Risk owner:
Context (supporting information):	

Figure 2.7 Example of a risk statement

the circumstances, contributing factors, and the related issues (or background and any other additional information you may deem appropriate).

2.7 Risk reviews

Project risk management should be viewed from two perspectives, that is short-term and long-term views. Short term will usually address the current project phase and immediate future. Whilst the long term by definition will address issues that are beyond the short term. Like many other aspects of risk management, the distinction between the two perspectives can sometimes be unclear to the project manager and the team. For clarity the short-term perspective normally refers to managing risk related to satisfying the immediate needs of the project, for example dealing with third party suppliers or dealing with performance issues during implementation. The long-term outlook deals with issues relating to what can be done to ensure that the project will be successful. This may involve amongst other things undertaking regular reviews of key risk statements.

2.7.1 Undertaking walkthroughs

A good way of conducting reviews is to hold regular walkthroughs of your key risk statements with key stakeholders. The purpose for conducting a walkthrough is to discuss key issues and spot errors of judgement as quickly and economically as possible. Generally speaking, it is more cost effective to mitigate risk as early as possible, rather than waiting until a project phase has been finished and sent on to the next stage of development.

When consulting on any risk issue, although you should be in listening mode, what people tell you will depend very much on how you pose the questions. Generally speaking, avoid imposing your own view of the issue, or inviting a particular response. It is good practice to ask questions differently to different stakeholders, and see if and how this alters the response. It is best not to presume that each stakeholder thinks about issues in the same terms as you – they do not. Try to be responsive to and show respect for individuals' attachment to establish ways to control risks, particularly if you are proposing the possibility of significant change. Remember people often feel threatened by what they don't understand or know. Try to establish a dialogue with people rather than an exchange in which all they receive from you are standard statements and e-mails. Be aware of the limitations of different ways to ask people about their views.

Going back to the mechanics of undertaking walkthroughs, with respect to risk a walkthrough is concerned with stepping through individual risk statements in an attempt to identify key issues with the objective of improving the delivery and quality of a particular project. Walkthroughs can be performed without training or formal procedures; however, it is often the case that it helps to introduce some formalism or structure to the review process.

As with any review, it is important to adopt the right attitude to a structured walkthrough. Specifically this requires commitment from both management and reviewers to ensure:

- Walkthroughs are scheduled in advance
- Adequate time is allowed for a review
- The necessary reviewers are available
- The review is effective.

Commitment is therefore required before, during and after the walkthrough. And each statement must be updated together with all agreed actions at the close of the meeting.

2.7.1.1 At what point

A risk walkthrough can take place at virtually any point in the life cycle of the project. In general it is preferable to have the first walkthrough as early as possible, but not so early that the project is incomplete or contains many trivial risks that the project manager could have removed or mitigated. The primary reason for avoiding a walkthrough at a late stage is that the project manager and the team may have invested so much of their time that he may be reluctant to make any changes in strategy. The project manager may also have needlessly wasted a lot of time detailing mitigation plans when the review team could have done it more quickly and economically if they had seen the strategy at an earlier point.

2.7.1.2 Participation

A common characteristic of a risk walkthrough is a set of formal roles that are played by the reviewers. Different reviewers can play different roles in different walkthroughs, or possibly play more than one. In any event the review team should be limited to six people. The exact make-up of the review team will be influenced by a number of considerations. Such considerations include:

- Complexity of the project
- Specialist domain knowledge
- Stakeholder politics
- Size of project team
- Use of third party suppliers.

In software projects typical participants in a risk walkthrough include:

- The project manager
- The senior user (or client)
- The technical architect (or senior designer)
- The lead analyst
- The test manager
- The implementation manager (or transition manager).

2.7.1.3 Formal process

Risk walkthroughs are generally characterized by a process supported by a set of formal roles and procedures. Procedures will vary from organization to organization; however, the following list is typical:

1 In advance of the review the project manager will distribute the risk documentation to the team of reviewers. Depending on the size of the document and other pressures upon personnel, distribution can vary before the review. Sufficient time must be given for the reviewers to be able to read through the material and to prepare themselves for the walkthrough.

2 The project manager should ensure that the reviewers have indeed spent some time reviewing the documentation. One easy way of doing this is to ask each reviewer to bring to the walkthrough at least one positive comment and one negative comment about the project.

3 If a third party presenter is being used ask the presenter to make a brief presentation of the project. This is where the group literally walks through the project.

4 Obtain comments from the reviewers. This is normally undertaken by the project manager, who may decide to go around the room, asking each reviewer in turn to point out a key risk or make a comment about the project.

5 Ensure that the issues are presented, but not resolved in the walkthrough.

6 If possible keep the walkthrough relatively brief – no more than half a day.

7 Take a consensus on the results of the walkthrough meeting. For example, recommendations that could be made by walkthrough reviewers are:

- We believe the project risk profile is OK.
- We believe some issues should be addressed immediately, but we trust the team to make the appropriate mitigation plans without any further reviews.
- We have found a sufficient number of risks and issues that we would like to have another walkthrough when the project manager has formulated the appropriate mitigation plans. For example, it is sometimes obvious from the outset of the project that there is a major risk to the project, which means that it has to be extensively managed. In these circumstances it is better to hold frequent reviews and schedule such reviews in the plan until the risk is no longer seen as a risk.

At the planning phase it is usually prudent to allow at least three reviews per stage of SDLC; risk walkthroughs can take up as much as 10 per cent of the total project's time.

2.8 Risk ownership and stakeholder management

Ownership of risk is a model of many dimensions and interpretations. The most important aspect of ownership is a clear mutual understanding of the responsibilities amongst stakeholders to a risk contract and responsibilities amongst stakeholders to a project. The second most important aspect is for a similar understanding on an intra-organizational basis.

In Chapter 1, point 1.5.1.2 we discussed in brief the identification and importance of stakeholder groups. I would like to expand on this subject further by exploring the need for stakeholder participation in the management of project risk.

There are many reasons to believe that adoption of a stakeholder approach to risk management and project management in general will contribute to the long-term survival and success of a project organization. Positive and mutually supportive stakeholder relationships encourage trust, and stimulate collaborative efforts that lead to positive teamwork.

Theorists emphasize that evaluation of stakeholder participation is:

- Concerned with processes which are qualitative and not results that are quantitative
- More concerned with description and interpretation than with measurement and prediction.

The measurement of participation requires:

- Valid criteria for understanding the nature of participation in a project
- A set of indicators to give form to these criteria
- Appropriate methods at project level for monitoring the indicators and maintaining a continuous record of the process of participation
- Interpretation of the information recorded in terms of making a judgement concerning participation.

Because traditional monitoring and evaluation has been concerned with quantifiable measurements, there is a new focus on the qualitative aspects of participation and on the process of participation. However, both qualitative and quantitative aspects of participation are important.

This requires two forms of monitoring and evaluation:

- Measurement based on numerical values leading to judgement
- Description leading to interpretation.

Because participation is a dynamic process that must be evaluated over time, conventional *ex post* evaluations are inadequate. Ongoing monitoring is the only way qualitative descriptions can be obtained over time. It should be participatory, involving the key personnel involved in the project.

Key characteristics to this qualitative approach to evaluating stakeholder participation are described as:

- Naturalistic: a study of processes rather than on the basis of predetermined and expected outcomes.
- Heuristic: subject to continuous redefinition as knowledge of a project and its outcome increase.
- Holistic: viewing the project as a whole, needing to be understood from many different perspectives.
- Inductive: seeking to understand outcomes without imposing predetermined expectations or benchmarks. It begins with specific observations and builds towards a general pattern of outcomes.

The steps involved are:

- Collecting the data and information that will reflect the process of participation during the lifetime of the project; and
- Analysing this data and information and making some form of judgement on the participation that has occurred.

(Clayton, Oakley and Pratt 1998)

2.8.1 Participation matrix

Projects are often at risk because the various stakeholders have different and conflicting expectations about their roles. The participation matrix is a dynamic tool, which provides a means for identifying potential areas of disagreement between the various stakeholders. Stakeholders have varying degrees of power and access to resources; some may lack the organizational basis for negotiation – indeed, at the identification stage of a project intended beneficiaries may not even be aware that they are stakeholders in the project. The participation matrix is likely to be used at the negotiation stage between the provider project manager and perhaps only some of the concerned formal stakeholder groups on the recipient side, with informed guesswork about the possible type of participation from beneficiaries and other institutions. But agreement as to how to include these other stakeholders so that they can be involved, as appropriate, in subsequent negotiations is essential. For example, in *bid or tender* related work this may often mean funded activities to enable less powerful stakeholders to organize and equip themselves for negotiations (McManus 2002).

2.8.2 Importance

When assessing the importance of stakeholders to a project's success, the use of 'checklist' questions is a good way of structuring thoughts and obtaining answers to which policy or strategy may be developed. For example:

- Which problems, affecting which stakeholders, does the project seek to address or alleviate?
- For which stakeholders does the project place a priority on meeting their needs, interests and expectations?
- Which stakeholder interests converge most closely with policy and project objectives?

As alluded to, assessing influence is often difficult and involves interpretation of a range of factors. By way of example, some of the factors that may be involved are illustrated in Figure 2.8.

Within and between formal organizations	For informal interest groups and primary stakeholders
Legal hierarchy (command and control, budget holders)	Social, economic and political status
Authority of leadership (formal and informal, charisma, political, familial or cadre connections)	Degree of project organization, consensus and leadership in the group
Control of strategic resources for the project (e.g. suppliers of hardware or other inputs)	Degree of control of strategic resources significant for the project
Possession of specialist knowledge (e.g. engineering staff)	Informal influence through links with other stakeholders
Negotiating position (strength in relation to other stakeholders in the project)	Degree of dependence on other stakeholders assessing importance to project success

Figure 2.8
Variables affecting stakeholders

2.8.3 Stakeholder impact

So what impact do stakeholders have on projects when it comes to risk? In essence they can have both a positive and a negative impact on projects. One of the most common ways of examining the impact of stakeholder participation on risk and project management is through previous projects or case studies. Sometimes these case studies are based on project appraisal and/or evaluation documents. One approach is to analyse why projects were not as successful as expected and to deduce where participation of stakeholders, particularly in the design and implementation stages, might have helped avoid some of the mistakes made.

Going back to the case research that the Standish Group did (in Chapter 1) on why projects fail, the group surveyed IT executives for their opinions about why projects succeed. The three major reasons why a project will succeed are user involvement, executive management support, and a clear statement of requirements. Without them, the chances of failure increase dramatically. Another key finding of the survey is that a high percentage of executive managers believe that there is more project failure attributed to stakeholder mismanagement than any other factor. For example, the survey identifies the following attributes as major challenges:

- Lack of user involvement
- Lack of resources
- Unrealistic expectations
- Lack of executive support
- Lack of IT management
- Unclear objectives.

To this list I would add the following:

- Continuous communication
- Trust and a good rapport
- Quick identification of problems (and presentation of options)
- Consideration to client needs and ideas.

To confirm these points, consider a case concerning the California Department of Motor Vehicles (DMV). The DMV embarked on a major project to revitalize their driver's licence and registration application process. After $45 million had already been spent, in 1993 they cancelled the project.

According to a lessons learned report issued by the DMV, the primary reason for redeveloping this application was the adoption of new technology. They publicly stated: 'The specific objective of the project was to use modern technology to support the DMV mission and sustain its growth by strategically positioning the DMV data processing environment to rapidly respond to change.' Also, according to the DMV special report 'The phasing was changed several times, but the DMV technical community was never truly confident in its viability.'

The project had no monetary payback, was not supported by any of the key stakeholder groups, including executive management, had no user involvement and unclear objectives. It also did not have the support of the state's information management staff. Because of internal state politics, unclear objectives and poor planning, the project was doomed from the start.

2.8.4 Argument

The argument of this lessons learned report is that the lack of support from stakeholders forced the project into disarray. Why? Because the majority of projects are not self-contained or self-sufficient, the stakeholder groups must be relied upon to provide support. For continuing to provide what the project needs, the external stakeholders may demand certain *quid pro quo* from the project in return. In short, it is the dependence of the project on external stakeholders for favours (and resources) that gives those individuals involved leverage over a project.

In applying this leverage, power and influence play a large part. Power can be defined as 'the structural determined potential for obtaining favoured payoffs in relations where interests are opposed'. Power is structurally determined in the sense that the nature of relationship is who is dependent on whom and how much determines who has power. Going back to the DMV case, there is some evidence to suggest that the project manager did not have the influence or power over key stakeholders. Initially the problems stemmed from poor perception and political issues that damaged relationships with the external stakeholder community which were not addressed early in the project life.

2.8.5 Expectations

In the world of projects and risk management, it is perhaps true to acknowledge that it is highly unlikely that all stakeholders' expectations will be met. Therefore, the project organization must somehow ascertain which stakeholders should be satisfied. Since stakeholders have the ability to positively or negatively influence the project, integrating the right group is essential. Specific organizational and project strategies used to integrate stakeholders will differ, depending on the issue and the group's potential to co-operate or threaten the firm's performance. Using the influencing model described in Figure 2.9 is a good starting point. In developing strategy, the project organization needs to consider that each stakeholder has the ability to both threaten and co-operate – the objective of the game is to reduce the threatening element and increase the co-operative behaviour of the stakeholder.

It is important to realize that the stakeholder's potential to act and their willingness to act are not directly related. Therefore, when looking at strategies, it is important to examine not only strategies addressing stakeholders who are positively disposed towards a project but those who are negatively disposed towards a project as well. Some strategies may only be appropriate for a stakeholder with a specific disposition towards the project, that is, positive or negative. In other cases a given strategy may be appropriate for either type of stakeholder.

2.9 Self-assessment checklist

Ask yourself	Yes	No	Not sure
Methods			
• Does the project team have a good understanding of the key project deliverables and life cycle development methodology?	☐	☐	☐
• Do the project team members have a good understanding of project risk?	☐	☐	☐
• Are the project team members familiar with qualitative methods of risk management? And, Are they trained in such methods?	☐	☐	☐
• Does the project manager have the freedom and ability to act when warranted?	☐	☐	☐
Risk classification			
• Does the project manager have a method for classifying risks?	☐	☐	☐
• Are these methods adequate?	☐	☐	☐
• Have all known management and technical risks been identified?	☐	☐	☐
• Have all known risks been mapped?	☐	☐	☐
• Are risk mapping tools being used? If so are they adequate?	☐	☐	☐
• Have key personnel been trained in the use of such tools?	☐	☐	☐
Risk statements and reviews			
• Is there formal agreement on which risks need reviewing?	☐	☐	☐
• Have risk statements been produced for all key risks?	☐	☐	☐
• Has the project manager reviewed these statements?	☐	☐	☐
• Is there a formal process for undertaking walkthroughs?	☐	☐	☐
• Have formal walkthroughs been arranged?	☐	☐	☐
• Are the reviews being held as scheduled?	☐	☐	☐
• Did the reviewers provide the necessary input to the risk review process?	☐	☐	☐
• Have actions been noted and have minutes been produced and circulated?	☐	☐	☐
• Have risk owners been identified and notified?	☐	☐	☐
Stakeholders			
• Has the project manager drawn up a list of key project stakeholders?	☐	☐	☐
• Has the project manager identified their level of authority and potential involvement in the project by means of a participation matrix?	☐	☐	☐
• Has the project manager arranged a stakeholder meeting to discuss key project issues?	☐	☐	☐
• Is the project manager managing stakeholder relationships within the domain of risks?	☐	☐	☐
• Does the approach to stakeholder management pass reasonableness checks in terms of what is to be accomplished?	☐	☐	☐

3   Risk assessment in software development projects

3.1 Recap on Chapter 2

From the previous chapter you will have ascertained the importance of having a clearly defined methodology for identifying and classifying risks. You will have also gained some insight into the qualitative tools used in the process of identifying risk, especially the use of the risk taxonomy method and risk mapping process.

The purpose and value of risk statements, the need for constant reviews during the software development life cycle and the process by which formal risk reviews are undertaken were discussed. Finally, we looked at the need for stakeholder involvement in the risk process and the importance of stakeholder participation.

It is perhaps worth stating at this point that risk management should be considered a core competency from which the project organization derives many of its competitive advantages. The ability to analyse, assess, measure and manage risk should be a prime concern in all the organization's business and technical decisions. Sensitivity to risk management innovations and issues should be seen as an integral part of the culture. Four principles guide the management of risk:

1 An organization-wide commitment to effective risk management starts at the senior management level.
2 A strong, centralized and independent control function for risk management operating in conjunction with decentralized

business activities enables the organization to be agile and efficient in its business activities, yet prudent in its overall risk taking.

3 Diversification is an efficient mechanism for managing risk.

4 Returns earned must be commensurate with the marginal risk associated with each business activity.

In this chapter we will explore the key aspects of risk assessment and expand on some of the material discussed in Chapter 2 and the points raised above.

3.2 Objectives and goals of software risk assessment

In Chapter 2 the process of defining risks was described in some detail. Having defined the risks associated with the project the next stage in the process is to ascertain what impact these risks will have on the project. From the risk statements and reviews we will have acquired some knowledge of the impact these risks may have on the project during its development life cycle (see points 2.6 and 2.7). A successful risk assessment effort depends on accurate information fed into the risk management process, which aids and provides guidance for decision making.

The scope of the assessment stage of the risk management process comprises:

1 Defining a baseline, that is what is the project's current picture and what defines its success?

2 The assessment of the likely outcomes of allowing the project to go forward on the basis of its present risk status

3 The establishment of a clear picture of the issues faced in these key areas (that is what can go wrong and what are the consequences)

4 The description of the extent of current risk reduction action and the diagnosis for improving risk reduction

5 Providing actions plans for risk reduction, which will involve:

- Mitigation and planning strategies to reduce or remove the effects of a realized risk
- Contingency planning, that is putting in place processes and resources to respond to the effects of a realized risk
- Fallback position, that is putting in place alternative business and technical strategies, untouched by the identified risk, which can replace that threatened should the risk be realized

- Transferring risk, that is the passing of risk to the other areas of the organization which are perhaps better placed to address it.

These points will be discussed in detail in the next chapter.

According to Karl Wiegers the skilful project manager will use risk management as a technique for raising the awareness of conditions that could cause the project to fail. For example, consider a project that begins with an unclear product vision and a lack of customer involvement. The astute project manager will spot this situation as posing potential risks, and will undertake an assessment of them. At the requirements stage the impact of this situation may not be too severe. However, if time continues to pass and the lack of product vision and customer involvement are not improved, the potential threat to the project will steadily rise and jeopardize the whole project. Under such circumstances assessment is paramount to success.

3.3 Approach to assessment

From our previous discussions in Chapters 1 and 2 we defined risk as three broad categories:

1 Category business risk: whatever affects your ability to meet project objectives. These risks are managed by the business and cannot be transferred.
2 Category technical risk: includes full SDLC project risk; these are managed by the party best placed to do so. Project personnel and stakeholders share detailed plans for managing risks.
3 Category external risk: outside the control of the project, such as legislation, changes in provider marketplace. Project personnel and stakeholders produce and maintain plans for mitigating these risks.

Through the preparation of risk statements (and supporting information), and perhaps the use of qualitative techniques we will have ascertained some view as to what our exposure to risk represents. Risk exposure helps us to list the risks in priority order, with the risks of most concern given the highest priority. The key activities associated with undertaking a risk assessment are listed below:

- Risk analysis, that is deciding the impact of the risk were it to occur, using predefined methods and techniques

- Risk prioritization, that is deciding which risks are important (*and why*)
- Risk mitigation, that is deciding on an appropriate course of action.

3.3.1 Key inputs

To carry out the activities listed above, the project manager and the team need various inputs in the form of documentation, methods and resources. As a minimum the following are required:

- Statements of risk (including any critical assumptions)
- Supporting documents (checklists, etc.)
- Access to stakeholders
- Access to tools
- Access to methods
- Access to funds.

First, no method of risk assessment is any better than its input. Second, the methods must be communicated and understood by experts and laymen alike. You analyse the risks you have identified, so that you can understand as much as possible about when, why and where they might occur. There are many methods, tools and techniques you can use to enhance your understanding including those listed in point 1.3.2.

3.4 Risk assessment tools and techniques

Organizations measure different risks using different tools. For example, organizations will employ software engineering techniques to highlight exposures, leading to maximum foreseeable risk. Project managers' projections are used for expected risk levels where sufficient data are available. Scenario analyses and Monte Carlo simulations are used when data are thin, especially to answer 'what if?' questions. Probabilistic and quantitative risk assessments are used for taxonomy estimates related to the SDLC, and to support stakeholder or policy decisions. For political risks, managers rely on qualitative analyses of 'experts'. When it comes to business risks (market, business cases, budgets, and costs of financing projects), we can be inundated with complex models that are comprehensible only to the initiated. The qualitative methods lack mathematical rigour and that leaves us with the quantitative tools that are often too abstract for laymen to understand, but which are nevertheless essential techniques in the risk tool box. However, if laymen can't understand the methods we employ, then we face the chance that it will be interpreted only by the 'technical experts', putting decisions squarely in the wrong hands. This could be considered by stakeholders to be an abrogation of senior management responsibility.

In essence organizations should use a combination of both tools so that they can deliver sensible and practical assessments of their risks to their stakeholders. For example, the project board, key users, project members, contractors, external customers, suppliers, regulators, and, finally, the user communities where operations occur. As previously discussed in point 2.8, each stakeholder group has a different perspective on risks, possible outcomes, and desired responses. Each group requires a different description that will enable us to communicate effectively with these various stakeholders?

3.4.1 Quantitative tools

I would now like to discuss some of those quantitative tools previously identified in point 1.3.2. Starting with symbolic models.

3.4.1.1 Symbolic models

Symbolic models some times termed abstract models make use of mathematical and statistical statements to present the problem under analysis. Symbolic models take the form of mathematical relationships that reflect the problem structure and behaviour. Symbolic models are generally used when the problem is complex and there are a number of interrelationships (that is risk dependencies), see Figures 3.1 and 3.2.

The main advantage of using symbolic models is the ease with which they can be manipulated and the fact that they yield accurate results. Some advantages to be gained from using symbolic models are:

- They assist in understanding the problem.
- Models can be more easily manipulated and analysed than a real system.
- They provide an indication of the information flow – and the gaps therein.
- Model building is an aid to decision making – a tool to help managers to decide what questions to ask themselves.

(Eden, Jones and Sims 1979)

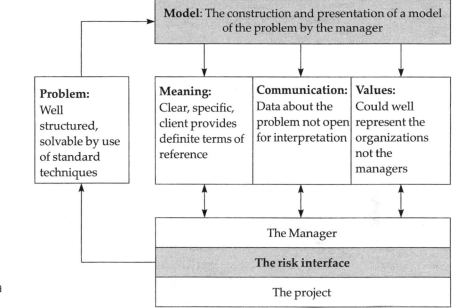

Figure 3.1
Characteristics of a model

Model	Advantages	Disadvantages
Simple computer models	• Low cost • Often simple to use • Can incorporate project-specific factors	• Likely to give conservative results • May not address all consequences • Some may not be simple to use
Complex computer models	• Address a variety of scenarios • Likely to consider many project-specific factors	• Likely to be costly • Likely to require a high level of expertise
Non-computer models	• Low cost • No computer requirements	• Likely to require expertise to apply methods • Likely to require development of a variety of data

Figure 3.2 Considerations for choosing a modelling method

3.4.1.2 Probability analysis

A decision is made under risk when the decision maker can assess, either intuitively or rationally, the probability of a particular event occurring, the probabilities of the event being based upon historical data or experience. Many project managers are by nature optimistic; however, an important source of bad decisions is fairly often illusions of certainty.

The computation of risk firmly requires the use of probability data. Probability values must either come from *real world* measurements, a validated model, or other convincing sources. Since uncertainty does exist, it is important that all known risks involved in making a decision are evaluated. Probability theory has often been referred to as the science of uncertainty. The use of probability theory allows the use of only limited information to analyse the risks and minimize the gamble inherent in building a new software system.

Events and probability

An event is a concept used by mathematicians in deriving their theory of probability. In simple terms an event is something which may or may not happen. For example, the software contract market may expand, or the repair cost of hardware may be higher next year. Given that the whole point of probability theory is to contend with situations in which events might happen rather than with situations in which events are certain to happen, it is usual also to describe what happens if an event does not occur. We therefore need to allow for two events, namely:

A, the contract market expands
B, the contract market retracts

If we are certain that an event will happen then its probability is expressed as 1.00. If the event is certainly not to happen then its probability is given as 0.00. If we think an event may happen then the probability will be somewhere between 0.00 and 1.00. The closer the probability is to 1.00 the greater the degree of expectation of the event occurring, for example the probability that the contract market will expand can be written as:

$P(A) = 0.70$

Where P stands for the probability of the event to which the probability statement refers to – the contract market expands is written in shorthand form in brackets (A).

Conditional probability

In many cases events do not happen by themselves but are dependent on other events taking place. For example, if the event A is the software is faulty and event B is the software program was found to have defects, then event A will depend to some degree on event B, that is event A is conditional on event B.

Conditional probabilities are often written in shorthand format as $P(X/Y)$. This is read as the probability of X given that Y has happened. For example, it was found that in a software package, 40 per cent of the product's functionality had software bugs. This statement can be abbreviated to read:

Let A denote event failed user test and B the event had software defects, therefore:

$$P(B/A) = 0.40$$

3.4.1.3 Consequence analysis

Consequence analysis was primarily developed as a tool to estimate the magnitude of effects related economic losses, or environmental impacts associated with accidents involving hazardous materials, etc., but is today used by many organizations involved in defining the consequences of risk.

Often, organizations dealing with hazardous situations run into questions that can't be answered any other way. For example, a consequence analysis is the best tool for getting answers to questions like:

- Will this mitigation system work?
- My emergency response plan didn't work when I needed it. What went wrong?
- After having been audited I have tens of outstanding recommendations. How can I possibly deal with so many?

The technique explores time sequenced system responses to initiating challenges to enable probability assessments to be made of success or failure (risk) outcomes. Such challenges might, for example, include software system failure or heightened business competition.

Consequence may be defined as: an array of outcomes representing staged increments of success/failure, with each increment having an associated level of probability, based on permutations of behaviour available within the system analysed (Clemens and Jacobs Sverdrup 2002).

The method involves undertaking an initial assessment of events and potential problems (causes) and then analysing the consequences, see Figure 3.3.

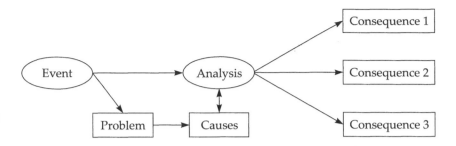

Figure 3.3
Representation causal analysis

The reported advantages of this method can be summarized as:

- Multiple outcomes are analysed
- Graduations of success and failure are distinguishable
- Single points of success and failure can be identified
- Zero payoff system components are identified
- End events need not be foreseen.

3.4.1.4 Decision tree analysis

As noted in Chapter 2, most organizations use some type of structured problem-solving process. Most problem-solving models include the following steps:

- Identify problems
- Identify a broad array of alternative courses of action
- Identify objectives and values to be taken into account
- Gather information relevant to the choices to be made
- Evaluate the alternatives
- Select the best alternative given the identified objectives and values
- Implement the decision
- Evaluate its execution to identify any further problems.

Decision tree analysis (DTA) is basically an extension of this type of problem-solving process. Decision trees offer a specific structure for exploring alternative courses of action to resolve a conflict. They are commonly used in business to evaluate various courses of action: for example, should the organization invest in projects or use its funds for some other activity such as product development. Generally, these types of decisions are based on monetary factors. However, non-monetary factors such as emotions, values, communication, and relationships can also be factored into DTA. For project managers, these soft factors are often more important than monetary ones.

Decision tree analysis follows six basic steps:

1 Depict the decisions to be made and possible outcomes for each decision
2 Assign probabilities to each of the uncertain events
3 Assign values to each of the possible outcomes
4 Calculate the expected values for each possible alternative
5 Identify soft factors that are relevant to the decisions to be made
6 Decide upon the best alternative.

Let us consider the information below. Suppose the organization has the choice of investing in a replacement software project which offers an overall profit of £1 million if successful, but a loss of £500 000 if unsuccessful. Alternatively the organization could choose to do nothing and use existing facilities which offer a profit of £300 000. What should it do? Based on the information below it should choose to undertake the project.

| Payoff matrix for Project Orange | | Optimum payoff | |
State	Probability	Undertake	Abandon
Project successful	0.60 (A)	1000 000	300 000 (Y)
Project unsuccessful	0.40 (B)	−500 000	300 000 (Z)
Expected payoff = (AY) + (BZ)		4000 000	300 000

Decision tree analysis does have a few drawbacks and limitations. First, decision trees and calculations can become cumbersome in complex situations. If there are many choices and possible outcomes, you may need to simplify the facts in order to make the analysis manageable. This may not reflect the full reality of the situation. On the other hand, decision trees help decision makers cut through complex details and focus upon the most important issues. Computer software designed to illustrate

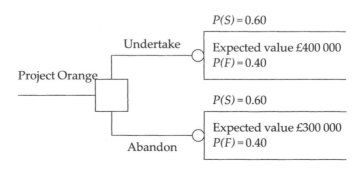

Figure 3.4
Example of a simple decision tree

decision trees and calculate expected values makes it easier to depict and synthesize complex situations.

Decision trees are useful because they:

- Clarify the decisions to be made
- Help to brainstorm alternatives in a structured manner
- Indicate the possible outcomes of alternate courses of action
- Identify factors that are critical to decision making
- Encourage the decision maker to consider rational factors as well as emotions, traditions, and moral sentiments
- Provide visual representations to guide the decision-making process, enabling one to see both the broad picture and the finer points.

3.4.1.5 Monte Carlo analysis (or simulation)

In 3.4.1.1 we discussed the use of models and how project models are used to forecast the behaviour of the project as a system. Monte Carlo analysis (MCA) is perhaps the easiest and most useful way to incorporate details about uncertainties. MCA, for example, allows distributions to represent activity time estimates and other uncertain inputs. Simulation can, for example, solve the project schedule, providing distributions and values for items such as time to complete and cost.

Monte Carlo analysis was named after Monte Carlo, in Monaco, where the primary attractions are casinos containing games of chance. Games of chance such as roulette wheels and dice exhibit random behaviour.

The random behaviour in games of chance is similar to how MCA selects variable values at random to simulate a model. When you roll a die, you know that a 1, 2, 3, 4, 5, or 6 will come up, but you don't know which for any particular roll. It's the same with the variables that have a known range of values but an uncertain value for any particular time or event (for example, resourcing requirements, software bugs, cash flows, etc.).

For each uncertain variable (one that has a range of possible values), you define the possible values with a probability distribution. The type of distribution you select is based on the conditions surrounding that variable. Types of distribution include:

- Normal distribution (the normal (or Gaussian) distribution is frequently encountered not only because it is a fundamental probability distribution function (pdf) for many physical and mathematical applications, but also because it plays a central role in the estimation of errors with MCA)

- Triangular distribution
- Uniform distribution
- Log-normal.

Using MCA the project manager can forecast such elements as:

- The probability that an activity lies on the critical path (looking back from project completion)
- The distribution for time to complete the project or any milestone sequence of activities
- The distribution of project cost or, better, project value to the customer
- The project manager can perform cost/benefit analyses for stakeholder risk mitigation actions and for possible activity crashing efforts.

Given our definition of Monte Carlo, let's now describe briefly the major components of an MCA. These components comprise the foundation of most Monte Carlo applications, and the following sections will explore them in more detail. An understanding of these major components will provide a sound foundation for the reader to construct his or her own Monte Carlo method, although of course the physics and mathematics of the specific application are well beyond the scope of this chapter. The primary components of an MCA method include the following:

- Probability distribution functions (pdfs) – the physical (or mathematical) system must be described by a set of pdfs.
- Random number generator – a source of random numbers uniformly distributed on the unit interval must be available.
- Sampling rule – a prescription for sampling from the specified pdfs, assuming the availability of random numbers on the unit interval, must be given.
- Scoring (or tallying) – the outcomes must be accumulated into overall tallies or scores for the quantities of interest.
- Error estimation – an estimate of the statistical error (variance) as a function of the number of trials and other quantities must be determined.
- Variance reduction techniques – methods for reducing the variance in the estimated solution to reduce the computational time for MCA.

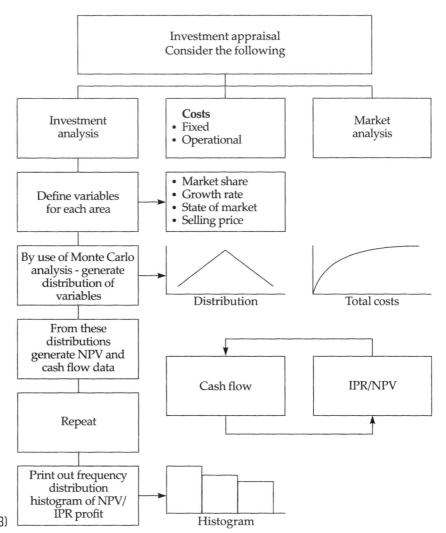

Figure 3.5

Pictorial view of the approach to Monte Carlo analysis (after Paul Harrison, © 1983)

- Parallelization and vectorization – algorithms to allow Monte Carlo methods to be implemented efficiently on advanced computer architectures.

Limitations

Some practitioners would argue that a whole host of issues and problems exist with quantitative risk methods. A number of limitations do exist using MCA for quantitative risk analysis. Interestingly there is no statistically sound basis to specify the commonly used triangle, beta or log-normal probability distribution for use in MCA.

Although a simulation technique, project managers and decision makers should recognize that an unknown level of uncertainty is often present which can substantially impact results. Correlations between risk analysis elements in the model in Figure 3.5 sometimes exist, but accurately modelling it is sometimes illusive.

3.4.1.6 Borda voting method

The Borda voting method is a quantitative risk management technique developed by a French mathematician in the late eighteenth century. The technique is used to rank risks from the most to the least critical on the basis of multiple evaluation criteria.

Borda proposed the method in 1770 and is explained as follows: Given N candidates, if points of $N - 1$, $N - 2$, ..., and 0 are assigned to the first-ranked, second-ranked, ..., and last ranked candidate in each voter's preference order, then the winning candidate is the one with greatest total number of points. Instead of voters, suppose that there are multiple criteria. If r_{ik} is the rank of alternative i under criterion k, the Borda count for alternative i is:

$$B_i = k (N - r_{ik})$$

The alternatives are then ordered to these counts.

The Borda method is an example of a positional voting method, which assigns Pj points to a voter's jth ranked candidate, $j = 1 \ldots, N$, and then determines the ranking of the candidates by evaluating the total number of points assigned to each item. Theorists have argued that the Borda method is the optimal positional voting method with respect to several standards, such as minimizing the number and kinds of voting paradoxes. If the ties are not present in the criteria rankings it is argued that the Borda method is equivalent to determining the consensus rankings that minimize the sum of the squared deviations from the criteria rankings.

The Borda method has been used successfully in a number of application development projects within the software and related industries.

3.4.1.7 Risk and investment decision making

As discussed, quantitative techniques endeavour to categorize the cost and risk associated with a system or proposed system. Costs may relate to the functions of the system, to those that are involved in the system or to the life cycle of the system. It is hoped that by careful cost analysis all sources of cost can be identified, and hopefully quantified, in a reasonably robust manner. IT project costs are extremely difficult to quantify. Some academics argue that no cost model can estimate the cost of software projects with any degree of certainty. While there is no real need to be this negative, it is acknowledged that in any reasonable cost model if it is applied as a standard across an organization it will probably be worthwhile; these comments do indicate the complexity of software cost decision making.

There is a strong correlation between cost overruns, risk and investment decisions. A survey of the IT literature indicates that the appraisal of IT projects is still a major concern for senior management of many large organizations. It is widely held that improvements in the processes of measuring IT costs, benefits and risks are the key to delivering successful projects, and for this reason I have decided to include a review of the techniques associated with financial appraisal of projects.

There are a number of techniques for assessing the value of investment decisions. The techniques require an estimation of all the costs and benefits (positive and negative) of a particular investment. The better known appraisal techniques are:

1 Payback method
2 Return on investment
3 Net present value
4 Discounted cash flow.

1. Payback method

Of the four methods this is the simplest and still one of the most popular (although some experts consider it worthless). The method is used to calculate the time period required to get back in cash the amount out laid on a project. Unlike the accounting rate of return method but like the discounting methods (3 and 4), it makes use of the incremental cash flow concept. Consider the information in Figure 3.6.

Some disadvantages

As mentioned earlier, this method concerns itself with cash flows but having defined these, it fails to make use of them. The method takes no account of earnings after the payback period. It also takes no account of the timing of receipts and payments.

Project	Red	Orange	Green
Investment	£20 000	£20 000	£20 000
Cash flows over 10 years	£30 000	£26 000	£25 000
Payback period	7 years	6 years	5 years
Payback profile	£2860 per year	£3334 per year	£4000 per year

Figure 3.6
Cash flow comparisons
(10 years)

Project Green achieves its payback during the course of the fifth year and would be preferred to Projects Red and Orange.

Despite these disadvantages, payback is widely used in making project investment decisions. The point must be made that payback can be used as a simple rough screening device for eliminating from consideration those projects which are not capable of yielding an adequate rate of return.

2. Return on investment

Return on investment is the ratio of profit to capital invested. The calculation is based on the total profit spread over the life of the project without reference to the pattern of earnings, that is whether early or late in the project life. For example, using the information contained in Figure 3.6:

Project	Red	Orange	Green
Average annual profits over 10 years	£3000	£2600	£2500
Return	15%	13%	12.5%

This method gives a different ranking from the payback method, placing Project Red first. This indicates that, if all of the original predictions and assumptions are correct, the initial capital investment of £20 000 will be recovered and additional dividends of 15% per annum will accrue each year over the 10 years the project is intended to run. Although this method is recognized by some of its adherents as an approximation to more refined methods, it is frequently justified on the grounds that it is sufficiently accurate for business and project managers.

The advantages are:

- It deals with profits and business managers are used to thinking in terms of profits.
- It takes account of profits during the project life cycle.

77

The method does have a number of disadvantages. These are:

- There are no universally accepted definitions of *capital invested or profit*, so that different people using the same basic data could report different rates of profitability. This might not matter provided the target rate had been established on the same basis as the project calculation.
- The method takes no account of the timing of payments and receipts. For example, profits earned in the earlier years are given equal weights with those earned in later years.

One point needs clarifying concerning the practical applications of the methods considered so far. That is cash flow. This is important, as cash available at a particular point in time is worth more than the same amount available 10 years later. This is because the amount available earlier can be put to use on other forms of investment. This is important because cash flows, which have been considered so far, should be subject to this type of consideration even though the fact has not been allowed for in the calculations. The time/cash flow relationship will be discussed now.

3. Net present value (NPV)

This method is used to compare project investments in a quantitative manner. A rate of interest is selected on which the calculations are based. This rate should normally be a rate that represents the cost of capital to an organization, or a rate that represents the minimum rate of return on capital acceptable to the organization. The cash flows expected over the life of a project are set down. They are then discounted at a selected rate of interest and the net present value of each cash flow item is obtained. The sum of these net present values gives the project its NPV.

Net present value can be used to take into consideration the *risk* associated with a project: the higher the perceived risk, the higher the discount rate applied, meaning that higher revenues are required to achieve a positive NPV. The formula for deriving the NPV of an investment is obtained from the general compound interest formula:

$$A = P(1 + R)^N$$

Where:

A = future value of capital invested
P = present capital invested
R = rate of interest (discount rate)
N = number of years during which the capital is invested

Example

Consider an example that involves two alternative proposals, Project White and Project Black.

The basic information relating to the projects is shown in Figure 3.7.

The result of the calculation is that Project White, after allowing for repayment of the capital invested in it, will yield an NPV of £5923 (29.6 per cent), whilst Project Black yields an NPV of £10 873 (54.4 per cent). Although both projects yield positive NPV over the capital invested, it is the figure of £10 873 that would be used for comparison with NPV calculated for other projects.

Project		White	Black
Capital invested		£20 000	£20 000
Cost of capital		15%	15%

Summary Project White

Years	Cash flow	NPV factor @ 15%	Present value
0–7	£45 000	£5923	£29 923
		Present value	£29 923
		Cost of capital	£20 000
		NPV	£5 923
		Profitability index	1.296

Summary Project Black

Years	Cash flow	NPV factor @ 15%	Present value
0–7	£53 900	£10 873	£30 873
		Present value	£30 873
		Cost of capital	£20 000
		NPV	£10 873
		Profitability index	1.544

Figure 3.7 Illustration of NPV

NPV is regarded as the most theoretically correct approach to investment appraisal. It has two features, which are appealing in the context of IT projects. First, NPV allows for the benefits, which accrue slowly and are typically delayed from the initial investment to be evaluated. Second, it provides a clear structure, which can help in overcoming the political and overvalued claims that are sometimes attached to IT projects.

4. Discounted cash flow

This method is based on the proposition that the best investment is that from which the proceeds would yield the highest rate of compound interest in equating present value with future proceeds. In essence it relates cash flow to the cost of investment.

In the preceding method we evaluated various project cash flows by means of finding their NPV at a given rate of interest and comparing these values with capital outlays to determine whether or not a given investment is attractive. There will be occasions, however, when it is more useful to know the rate of interest that will equate capital outlays and their resultant cash flows. This rate of interest is known as the investment rate, or more commonly the yield rate. The yield rate is the solution to r to our second equation, where E is substituted for P:

$$E = \sum_{I = 1}^{I = N} = Ai/(1 + R)$$

Where:

E = the project expenditure
Ai = the project benefit measured at the end of the period
N = the expected project life (for example 10 years)
R = the rate of return to be established

An example of the calculation involved in the yield method for Project Brown is shown in Figure 3.8. Return on investment for 5 years is 16.6 per cent. Using this method any terminal value of subsequent income is ignored.

Project Brown capital expenditure	£50 000
Expected life of project	5 years
Cash flow over 5 years	£80 000
Discount rate between	16 and 17%
NPV between	£50 765 and £49 515
Interpolate discount rate	765/1250 = 16.6%

Figure 3.8
Illustration of yield method

The advantages of this method are:

- It takes into account the time value of money, that is the pattern of payments and savings, not merely the total. The time value of money in this context has nothing to do with inflation. We are talking about the cost of money, not its purchasing power. The effects of inflation must be forecasted and included in the cash flows before we start discounting them.

- It takes into consideration the full life cycle of the project.
- It enables a comparison to be made with the cost of capital.

The disadvantages of the method are:

- The micro nature of the calculations sometimes blinds project and business managers to the unreliability of the data on which they are based.
- There is sometimes a difference between the results obtained by the yield method and the NPV method and it is difficult to know when each should be used.

As a general guideline, however, if an organization is financially able to implement all projects that show a rate of return in excess of the cost of capital, and if the particular projects under investigation are not mutually exclusive, then either the yield method or NPV may be used. Project investment projects that show a higher yield than an organization's cost of capital or that have a positive NPV when discounted at the cost of capital are acceptable.

In summary, project managers often prefer simple answers to relatively complex questions and want to be able to compare different options easily. Of the four methods evaluated the first two suffer weaknesses particularly in that they do not take account of the effect of timing cash flows. The advantage of discounting methods is that they indicate the correct mathematical calculation necessary to show the true economic worth of a project (McManus 1981).

3.4.1.8 Cost–benefit analysis

Cost–benefit analysis is a systematic, quantitative method of assessing the life cycle costs, benefits and risks of competing alternative approaches. This includes determining which one of the alternatives is best and often goes hand in glove with the appraisal techniques previously discussed.

As previously discussed, project and other managers are often faced with alternative or difficult choices. In assessing alternative investment decisions the project must usually consider at least three alternative means of achieving project objectives, one of which is to continue with no change and this provides a comparative baseline. In a software project typical alternatives may include:

- In-house development versus offshore development
- In-house operation versus managed service operation
- Leasing equipment versus purchasing equipment
- Current operational procedures versus new operational procedures
- One technical approach versus another technical approach.

The process of undertaking a cost–benefit analysis (CBA) must include comprehensive estimates of the projected benefits, risks and costs for all alternatives. Benefits to which a value cannot be assigned should be included along with tangible benefits and costs. Intangible benefits should be evaluated and assigned relative numeric values for comparison purposes. For example, maximum benefit could be assigned a value of 10, average benefits a value of 5, and minimum benefits a value of 1. Evaluating and comparing benefits that have both £ values and relative numeric values require extra effort, but allow subjective judgement to be a factor in the analysis.

The process of undertaking a CBA involves the following steps:

- Determines objectives
- Documents current process
- Estimates future requirements
- Collects cost data
- Chooses alternatives
- Assesses risks
- Documents assumptions
- Estimates costs
- Estimates benefits (tangible and intangible)
- Discounts costs and benefits
- Evaluates alternatives
- Makes recommendation
- Adopts/rejects
- Manages risks.

The key to success in undertaking a CBA is in step one, the objectives; get this one step wrong and the remaining steps add no value whatsoever. CBA should include the project objectives and other pertinent background information so that it stands on its own and can be understood by a reviewer who is not intimately familiar with the project organization and its work process. The objectives should be designed to improve the work process so the organization can better perform its mission. The key items to be addressed in the CBA step one are:

Year	Start-up costs £s	Acquisition costs £s	Development costs £s	Operation costs £s	Maintenance costs £s	Total costs £s
1	200 000	500 000				700 000
2			1 800 000			1 800 000
3				300 000	50 000	350 000
4				300 000	50 000	350 000
5				300 000	50 000	350 000
6				300 000	50 000	350 000
7				300 000	50 000	350 000
8				300 000	50 000	350 000
9				300 000	50 000	350 000
10				300 000	50 000	350 000
Sub total	200 000	500 000	1 800 000	2 400 000	400 000	5 300 000

Figure 3.9 Annual cost matrix – 10-year IT development project

- Problem definition – the problem perceived by management must be clearly defined.
- Background – pertinent issues such as staffing, system history, risks, customer satisfaction should be addressed.
- Project objectives – the objectives should be stated in terms of supporting the project charter.

Although it is important for the reader to understand the project objectives, the crucial issue is that the project manager and management understand what it is that they are trying to accomplish. In some environments, a CBA may be initiated when management has only generally defined the problem. When that occurs, the time and effort that is required to complete the CBA is likely to be increased significantly.

All cost elements must be identified and estimated for each year of the system life cycle. This will be necessary for planning and budget considerations. Figure 3.9 illustrates estimated annual costs over the life of a 10-year IT project.

Benefits

Identifying and estimating the value of benefits will probably be the most difficult task in the CBA process. Benefits are the services, capabilities, and qualities of each alternative system, and can be viewed as the return from an investment. Webster uses such terms as advantage, useful aid, help, and service to define it. Some examples of benefits for IT systems are given below:

- Accuracy: will the proposed system provide better accuracy by reducing the number of data entry errors or eliminate some data entry that would, in turn, result in fewer data entry errors?
- Availability: how long will it take to develop and implement the system? Will one alternative be available sooner than others?
- Compatibility: how compatible is the proposed alternative with existing facilities and procedures? Will one alternative require less training of personnel or less new equipment or software?
- Efficiency: will one alternative provide faster or more accurate processing of inputs? Will one alternative require fewer resources for the processing?
- Maintainability: will the maintenance costs for one alternative be less than the others? Are the maintenance resources easier to acquire for one alternative? An example of this would be availability and cost of programmers to maintain the software.
- Modularity: will the software for one alternative be more modular than the other alternatives? Greater modularity can reduce maintenance costs and may increase the portability of the software.
- Reliability: does one alternative provide greater hardware or software reliability? Greater reliability translates to higher productivity in using and/or operating the system and less time for operations and user support.
- Security: does one alternative provide better security to prevent fraud, waste or abuse? Are privacy, confidentiality, and data integrity enhanced?

Every proposed IT project for an organization should have identifiable benefits for both the organization and its customers. Identifying these benefits will usually require domain knowledge and an understanding of the work processes of the organization and its customers. Typically, the benefits to the customers will be much less than the benefits for the organization that is developing the system. Possible benefits to customers may include improvements to the current IT services, reduction of risk and the addition of new services.

3.4.1.9 Quantitative market research

The use of market research (or intelligence gathering) to understand complex geographical markets and the risks involved in delivering information technology related products are playing an ever-increasing part in the management and delivery of product related projects. This is certainly true for those organizations that compete for business in the global market place. IT and other research institutions provide secondary data, that is white papers and reports on a host business and technological subject matter.

A use of market research is that such organizations can look into specific risks because they have the specialist knowledge – this is usually more cost-effective than engaging project staff who may have to go through steep learning curves to achieve the same result.

The use of secondary data offers two important advantages over that of primary organizational risk data:

1 The assembly of previously collected data is almost always less expensive than a collection of primary data.
2 Less time is involved in locating and using secondary data.

The project manager must be aware of two potential limitations to the use of secondary data:

1 The data may be biased, or
2 The data classifications may not be usable.

Data collection should be preceded by a detailed research design, which can be defined as a series of advanced decisions that, taken together, comprise a master plan or model for the conduct of the investigation. By developing a comprehensive plan for performing the study, the project manager can control each step of the investigation and can avoid potential problems at the outset of the study. The steps involved include:

- Decide the subjects on which data are needed
- Examine the time and cost considerations
- Write exact statements of data to be sought
- Search and examine relevant secondary data
- Identify gaps
- Plan for obtaining data
- Consider the questions and forms to elicit the data

- Map and schedule work, including personnel
- Anticipate possible interpretations of data
- Consider the way in which the findings may be presented.

Questions the project manager must consider:

- What data do I need to collect on risks?
- How should the data be obtained?
- How will the exercise be conducted?
- How will the results be interpreted?
- How will the results be used?

The project manager has three alternatives in the collection of primary data: observation, survey, or controlled experiment. No one method is best in all circumstances; in fact, any one may prove the most efficient in a particular situation.

Software vendors are usually happy to provide risk information on competitors because it gives them an opportunity to market their services. Be sure, however, to let them know you are only looking for data for planning and analysis purposes, and that no procurement is planned at the present time. Organizations such as the Gartner Group and government agencies can also provide assistance in developing risk data. A word of caution though, if you use a market research company, you generally get what you pay for – there is no such thing as a free lunch.

3.5 Presenting the findings

The purpose of risk assessment is to make better decisions about future actions in an uncertain environment; however, much of risk management is about understanding the potential for risks and their consequences, and potential is sometimes difficult to sell to senior managers. For example, when it comes to making value judgements about risks, for some, it will not be viable to impose a rationalized approach whatever its logical benefits. With this in mind the objective of using the qualitative and quantitative methods outlined in points 2.2 and 3.4 above is to assist the project manager in making decisions about prioritizing risks in terms of severity and potential impact on the project or organization.

To effectively compare identified risks, and to provide a proactive perspective, the method of prioritization should consider three factors:

1 The probability of the risk occurring
2 The impact of the risk
3 The exposure.

To recap from our discussions in Chapter 2, risk is composed of two factors, that is *risk probability* and *risk impact*. Risk impact measures the severity of adverse effects, or the magnitude of a loss, if the risk comes to pass. Deciding how to measure sustained losses is not a trivial matter. If the risk has a financial impact, a £'s value is the preferred way to quantify the magnitude of loss. The financial impact may be long-term costs in operations and support, loss of market share, short-term costs in additional work, or lost opportunity cost. Other risks can have a level of impact where a subjective scale from 1 to 5 is more appropriate. These essentially rate the viability of project success. High values indicate serious loss to the project. Medium values show loss to portions of the project or loss of effectiveness. To evaluate a list of risks, the overall threat of each risk needs to be clearly understood. Sometimes a high probability risk has low impact and can be safely ignored; sometimes a high impact risk has low probability and can be safely ignored as well. The risks that have high exposure (high probability and high impact) are the ones worth managing. Reducing either the risk probability or the risk impact can do this. When estimating probability and impact, be aware of what you know and what you don't know. If you think a risk could result in a significant £'s loss, but your level of confidence is 50 per cent, the people who are reviewing the risk analysis need to understand these factors.

3.5.1 Risk probability

Risk probability can be defined as the likelihood that this risk will actually happen. The most common notation is:

1 Almost certainly will not occur
2 Very unlikely to happen
3 Quite possible – it has happened on some previous projects
4 Probably will happen
5 Certainly will happen, no question.

Each risk identified is assigned an estimated probability of occurring during the course of the project to allow the project manager to be watchful for signs of its effects. A probability estimation must be recorded when a new risk is identified.

Again the most common approach is to assign the probability of the risk occurring a value between 0.00 and 1.00. For example:

0.00–0.10   Improbable: *very unlikely the risk will occur*
0.11–0.40   Remote: *unlikely the risk will occur*
0.41–0.60   Occasional: *even likelihood the risk will occur*
0.61–0.90   Probable: *likely the risk will occur*
0.91–1.00   Frequent: *very likely the risk will occur*

3.5.2 Risk impact

Risk impact is the consequence if this risk/threat were to actually happen. The most common notation is:

1 Almost *negligible* impact – can easily be rectified.
2 Would have *minor* effect on budget or schedule. Could take a few days to fix.
3 Noticeable and *moderate* effect on budget and schedule. Will require review of plan and some rescheduling.
4 Problem is *serious* which could affect credibility/integrity of project. May need to seek additional resources/funding. May require us to consider significant project reschedule.
5 Project failure *critical*. Likely to cause project to fail or be abandoned. Likely to cause costs or time estimates to be significantly behind.

All risks are also assigned an impact rating to act as a measure of how detrimental the risk is expected to be, should it occur. The impact of a risk must be decided when the risk is identified. The impact of the risk is usually given a value between 1 and 5. For example:

- The risk will delay progress of an individual task within the group — Assign value 1

- The risk will delay progress of the project slightly, probably localized to a group within the team — Assign value 2

- The risk will noticeably delay progress of the project, and may affect the entire team — Assign value 3

- The risk will affect the whole team's progress, and demands attention from the project manager — Assign value 4

- The risk will affect the whole team, and demands immediate and definite action from the project manager — Assign value 5

3.5.3 Risk exposure

Exposure is a value generated from the probability and impact assigned to a risk (as seen below). Large exposures indicate the risk is a much greater danger to the project, small exposures indicate that a risk is relatively unimportant, by and of itself. The exposure of a risk is used for ranking its importance and danger for the project or organization. Exposure of a risk is the product of probability and risk. That is: Exposure = Probability × Impact. Experience shows that risks that have the highest exposure should always have the utmost priority. Take the following scenario as an example: the project manager identifies three key risks, these are:

1 Poor strategic alignment of the project to client's business needs
2 Poorly defined software requirements
3 Insufficient business knowledge.

Using the exposure formula, Probability × Impact, the project manager considers risk exposure to be as below. The output from this process feeds the risk matrix in Figure 3.10 discussed next.

Risk	Probability	Impact	Exposure	Project manager's notes
Poor strategic alignment of the project to client's business needs	0.90	5	High	This is a serious risk to the project and requires urgent debate by the project board
Poorly defined software requirements	0.70	4	Medium	Any action is dependent on the above outcome
Insufficient business knowledge	0.70	4	Medium	Any action is dependent on the above outcome

3.5.4 Constructing a risk matrix

A risk matrix is a table used to assign a total to the identified risk, to assist with the risk management process. A typical risk matrix is a five by five grid, Figure 3.10 is a simplified example for the purpose of explanation.

89

Probability of occurrence		Risk impact				
		Negligible 1	Minor 2	Moderate 3	Serious 4	Critical 5
Improbable	0.00–0.10	Low	Low	Low	Medium	Medium
Remote	0.11–0.40	Low	Low	Medium	Medium	High
Occasional	0.41–0.60	Low	Medium	Medium	Medium	High
Probable	0.61–0.90	Medium	Medium	Medium	Medium	High
Frequent	0.91–1.00	Medium	High	High	High	High

Figure 3.10 Example of risk matrix

Construction of a risk matrix table starts by first establishing how the matrix will be used (and who will use it?), for example the project board may wish to review this matrix in association with the project manager before any key decisions are made. Once the probability and impact values have been determined, they can be written into the table to portray their relative importance and exposure to the project.

One problem with impact categories is that of having relative data to quantify the impact. Generally speaking, this involves determining the frequency of the initiating event and then determining the probability of all other events. Without extensive experience in quantitative risk assessment and a comprehensive database of failure rates, this becomes a judgement activity and may result in assigning impact categories to scenarios that are much lower than would be determined through quantitative risk assessment. When it comes to making value judgements the project manager must identify whose views and opinions really matter to those making the decision:

- Those affected by the risk
- Those who create the risk and/or will have to take action to manage it
- Those whose opinions, advice or behaviour will influence people's responses.

The project manager must be open about what is wanted and why? Do not pretend that your technical expert will lead you to decisions that satisfy everybody, but do let people know how you will use their input. Remember to thank individual team members for their input, and behave with respect for their opinions, whatever you may think of them.

Because risk assessment and the ranking of risk are considered by some to be a semi-quantitative tool, it might be seen as conformist and in some cases assign higher than actual impact categories to risk scenarios. In such cases the project board may choose to conduct a rigorous quantitative risk assessment to refine the numbers before investing considerable resources to mitigate risk.

Figure 3.10 allows the project manager to assess those risks with the highest project priority. If the project team constructed this table, the team should meet with the project manager to discuss the results (prior to developing a mitigation strategy) and achieve agreement on the top risks to be managed. In such circumstances decisions regarding how to handle the top risks will vary depending on stakeholder views or the opinion of the project board. Some risks will be eliminated because the political climate changes; others may be transferred within the organization or to external agencies if resources are an issue or because it's more appropriate for the client organization to handle them; for example, the problem with 'poor strategic alignment of the project to clients business needs' is one, others will require mitigation strategies. The risks that are not considered critical should be recorded and reviewed at regular intervals, ensuring adequate processes are in place to collect and act on feedback and on policy and actions.

3.5.5 Application problem

A recent article by David McNamee (2002) spells out the benefits of undertaking risk assessment. David's paper discusses the role of information systems auditing within a financial services company. Selected parts of the case are discussed below.

A few years ago, a financial services company formed an internal audit group to assist management with the evaluation of internal control. Within two years, the internal audit director realized that information system auditing was an important part missing from the current internal audit function. Information systems is an important part of their business, and yet there was no audit coverage. The internal audit director decided to develop a long-range IS audit planning project that included an update to the audit universe and a risk model to define the annual IS audit schedule.

The Mc^2 Management Consulting approach was to review a number of key business documents. We looked at business plans, annual reports, audit results, organization charts, and similar documents to piece together the basic building blocks of this company. Although geographically diverse, the company had only a few mainline business processes and product groups. At a high level, the processes themselves were not complex; however, integrating and consolidating these processes into a single entity report was very complicated. In addition to documentation, we interviewed senior management to test our understanding of the business purpose and business process.

By understanding the nature of the business through the structures the company had built and through the way people used the structures, we identified a number of risks. These risks are the uncertainties in the universe that can affect the company reaching its goals. We used the COSO approach to risk as a model: established objectives determine which risks are significant, and the risks determine which control activities to audit.

The generic risks to the business were:

- Loss of key assets, chiefly information, the network and skilled people (from various sources)
- Disruption of key processes, chiefly revenue and regulatory reporting (from various sources).

To help us identify and catalogue the key assets and key processes, we used a worksheet to map out the key items and the primary sources of risk. This worksheet mapped risk in terms of the assets at risk (financial, physical, human, and informational) as well as the various environments that could affect operations (competition, technology, customers, regulation, etc.). The sources of external or environmental risk were useful stimulators for thinking about risks that we might have excluded otherwise. Rather than focus too much on the various sources for the risks, we focused on the exposures or consequences of those risks to key assets and key processes. The IS assets and processes were classified into broad groups:

- Systems
- Projects
- Processes
- Server sites

Within these groups, we catalogued IS audit topics for inclusion in the audit universe.

The model

The interview process and the earlier work done to understand the business identified the major risks. We looked for clues in this summarization that would point to observable or measurable factors to serve as substitutes for the risk itself. We chose seven risk factors, and then we validated them with a number of people in the organization, including the internal audit director. The factors chosen were:

- Impact size
- Rate of change
- Business impact
- Complexity
- Recoverability
- Value
- Management team focus.

Using the seven risk factors, we set up two scoring teams for the IS audit universe: the risk model project team and a knowledgeable management team. Both teams independently scored each of the audit universe topics on a scale of 1 (low) to 5 (high). The risk model was an 'equal-weight' model, meaning that each factor had equal weight in the scoring system. Another approach could have been to adjust the model by giving certain factors more influence by assigning more weight, but the existing model in use was also equal weight. We used the same method so that we could integrate with the existing risk methodology.

We used a simple spreadsheet to capture the audit universe and the seven factor scores for each topic. It was easy then to sort the scores from highest to lowest. The existing risk model for non-IS audits used a cut-off score of 4.25 to mean high risk, and we stayed within that parameter for consistency with existing risk methodology. The teams compared scores and ranking, and the lists were nearly identical. The model worked!

The result was that the audit universe included the following IS audit topics as critical risk areas (approximately 27 per cent of all IS audit topics):

- Major server sites for the WAN
- Major financial applications systems conversion project
- Major network operating system conversion project
- IS network administration process
- IS applications development process
- Major financial consolidation applications (several)
- Major revenue applications (several).

By dedicating resources to this project full time, the internal audit director was able to produce a fully developed IS audit universe and risk model. The model met all of the constraints, and the team did it in less than two weeks (McNamee 2002).

3.6 Self-assessment checklist

Ask yourself	Yes	No	Not sure
Risk assessment approach			
• Does the project manager and project team know and understand the scope of the risk assessment process?	❏	❏	❏
• Does the project manager and project team agree on the approach to risk assessment?	❏	❏	❏
• Does the approach pass reasonableness checks in terms of what is to be accomplished by the process?	❏	❏	❏
• Have the project team been trained in quantitative methods of assessment?	❏	❏	❏
• Have the risks been identified and recorded?	❏	❏	❏
• Have key stakeholders participated in the identification process?	❏	❏	❏
• Have risks been categorized into groups, for example political, economic, technical and external?	❏	❏	❏
• Has the project manager gone to others in the organization for relevant knowledge and advice?	❏	❏	❏
• Is the likelihood of the risk occurring calculated for all risks?	❏	❏	❏
• Is the magnitude of the impact calculated for all risks identified?	❏	❏	❏
• Is the tolerance level for each risk determined?	❏	❏	❏
• Is the exposure level for each risk known?	❏	❏	❏
• Have the results been tabulated into a risk matrix?	❏	❏	❏
• Has the project manager reviewed the results?	❏	❏	❏
• Has the project board reviewed the results?	❏	❏	❏
• Has the project team received feedback from the project manager?	❏	❏	❏

<table>
<tr><td>**4**</td><td></td></tr>
</table>

Planning risk mitigation strategies in software development projects

4.1 Recap on Chapter 3

From the previous chapter you will have ascertained how important it is to supplement the qualitative methods of risk assessment with quantitative methods. Some project managers argue that quantitative methods of risk assessment are perhaps optional extras. I personally have never subscribed to this school of thought; my belief is that project managers should use all tools and methods available to them.

In reviewing the scope of the assessment stage of the risk management process we looked at:

- The objectives and goals within risk assessment
- The approach to risk assessment
- The key inputs to risk assessment
- The tools and techniques used within the risk assessment process.

In this chapter we will discuss the use of:

- Mitigation and planning strategies to reduce or remove the effects of a realized risk
- Contingency planning, that is putting in place processes and resources to respond to the effects of a realized risk
- Fallback position, that is putting in place alternative business and technical strategies, untouched by the identified risk, that can replace that threatened should the risk be realized
- Transferring risk, that is the passing of risk to the other areas of the organization who are perhaps better placed to address it.

4.2 Risk planning

We touched briefly on planning in Chapter 1 (refer to points 1.5.1.7 and 1.6.1.3). To recap the risk management planning process is extremely important for the positioning of risk management within the software development process. Clearly most practising project managers acknowledge the introduction of risk planning as absolutely crucial. Risk planning highlights the fact that risk management activities need to be planned, budgeted and have resources allocated to them. From our discussion in Chapter 1, we know that risk management can no longer be viewed as something that distracts the project manager from the important task of being an effective manager. Risk planning is at the core of the management activity, and should be considered to be both tactical and strategic in nature. Although risk planning may be considered tactical in nature it also serves as a strategic activity in that it allows senior managers to view many projects across the piece. In these circumstances risk planning becomes a strategic activity, covering many disciplines and environments. See Figure 4.1.

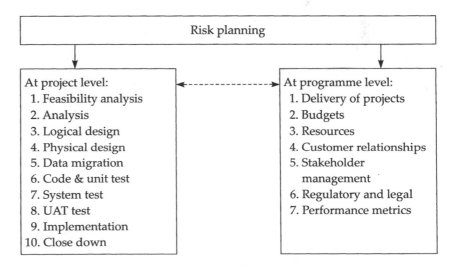

Figure 4.1
Risk planning

To begin development of an effective risk planning process that is both complementary and supportive of the project, the first step within risk planning is to define the objectives.

4.2.1 Risk planning objectives

The objective of the risk planning process is to achieve the best possible balance and efficiency in managing risk. A risk efficient process is one where the expected cost of mitigating the risk can only be decreased by increasing the likelihood or impact of the risk. It is the arbitrary balance struck between the organization's willingness to suffer the consequences of risk and its willingness to pay for its avoidance strategies and this is where risk planning helps. The goals of risk planning are identified as:

- Establishing priorities for risk reduction
- Identifying options for risk reduction action
- Identifying potential fallback positions
- Deciding which options to implement.

To ensure that the risk planning process is productive a number of inputs will be required. The project manager should prepare a risk pack – this risk pack should contain an official agenda together with:

- Risk statement information (see point 2.6)
- Risk review information (see point 2.7)
- Risk probability, impact and exposure information (see point 3.5)

When undertaking risk planning sessions it is sometimes considered appropriate to have a facilitator, that is someone who can act in an arbitrary position (similar to that of a JAD facilitator in development sessions). In addition to the goals stated above the risk planning sessions should aim to decide:

- The validity of risk – based on the risk statements
- Whether risks are considered short, medium or long term
- The accuracy of the risk as stated
- The true exposure to the project or business
- The true ownership of the risk (a risk owner should remain assigned to a risk until such a point that the risk has been reduced to such an extent that it no longer needs the concentrated effort of a risk owner – this should be the project manager's call)
- Plan for approval of risk reduction, further investigation or actions
- Plan for risk contingency (which includes asking questions such as: What are the conceivable effects if the potential problem occurs? How can we minimize the negative effects? How expensive are the contingency measures?)

In most medium sized software projects, there will be between 10 and 15 significant risks that should be prepared for during the planning phase. Simple questions such as, How do we minimize risks? and If something unplanned happens, what can be done to lessen the impact on the business? must be answered. For a software project manager, this may include identifying alternate suppliers that may be used if a key supplier cannot deliver on time, at a cost-effective price. Other risks to consider are loss of key personnel or simply not planning risk contingency.

4.2.2 Pre-planning meeting

Once the agenda is set it is useful to have a pre-planning meeting, that is a discussion with key members of the management team and other key personnel if appropriate. The purpose of this meeting is to ensure the agenda is pitched at the right level. Care must be used to be straightforward and honest but yet persuasive. The project manager should feel confident that the management team and key personnel are qualified to participate and subsequently do the jobs assigned to them. Pen profiles of the management team may be included in an appendix to the agenda and plan if appropriate.

4.3 Best practice in risk planning (and risk management)

What constitutes best practice in risk planning? This question is difficult to answer. Research would suggest, however, that the more time you allocate to risk planning and preparation of the plan, the greater your chances for project success and the greater the opportunities for success.

At this point I believe the discussion would benefit from a wider forum on what constitutes 'best practice'. Recent research points to a number of generic factors that facilitate good practice. These are defined as follows:

- Properly defined standards and adherence to such standards
- Continuous improvement in the practice of risk management
- Competent personnel trained in the use of risk management practices
- The use of risk and software metrics
- The use of risk management tools (see point 4.4).

4.3.1 Properly defined standards and adherence to such standards

The adoption of risk management and its resulting success in my experience relies to a large degree on the use and subsequent enforcement of standards whether commercial or bespoke. The key point here is not so much what standards are used (proprietary or bespoke) but the fact that standards are used. Adherence to standards breeds discipline and a sense of ownership.

There are of course many open standards that one can implement. Widely recognized standards in the UK include the British Standard BS6079 (Part 3 Guide to the management of business-related project risk) or the Association Project Manager's (APM) Project Risk Analysis and Management (PRAM) Guide. Other significant guidance documents include the Risk Analysis and Management of Projects (RAMP) Guide from ICE, or Management of Risk Guidelines from the OGC. It is perhaps worth pointing out that many of these give much the same advice, as we are now beginning to see some union amongst project managers on the required processes, tools, and techniques.

Other common international standards include the Australian/New Zealand Standard AS/NZS 4360, and Association of Project Managers (USA), Body of Knowledge (APM-BoK, 2000). British Standard BS6079 (Part 3 Guide to the management of business-related project risk) offers some sound advice on the management of project risk. The document is aimed at relative newcomers to project management and people who interact with projects who need to understand what project management risk is about. It is also seen as an *aide-mémoire* for more experienced project management personnel. It is written primarily for small to medium sized organizations, but is equally applicable for larger organizations.

The British Standard BS6079 1996, A Guide to Project Management, Section 4 (4.6.3 Risk Management) also contains generic information on risk management. This document, however, is not intended for formal conformance but it can be used for contractual arrangements. It uses a definition of project risk, taken from the international quality standard in project management, which includes the implementation and operational phases as part of the project life cycle.

4.3.1.1 Observation

If the risk planning phases of these standards are examined one may conclude that BS6079 Part 3 offers the most appropriate model for risk. The risk treatment phase within the process suggests dealing with risk under four headings:

1 Eliminating or avoiding risk
2 Risk sharing
3 Reducing the possibility
4 Reducing the consequences.

BS6079 also offers four options for addressing opportunities, namely:

1 Facilitating (choosing the project approach accordingly and enhancing other beneficial stakeholder outcomes)
2 Involving facilitators (involving stakeholders who can help facilitate occurrence of the opportunity)
3 Enhancing likelihood (changing the project approach, examining causal links between opportunity and project)
4 Enhancing consequences (developing plans for taking advantage of an opportunity if it occurs).

4.3.2 Continuous improvement in the practice of risk management

The aim of continuous improvement is to exploit gains made in knowledge acquisition and to ensure that such gains are fed back into the risk management process. The use of common risk management processes has several practical advantages, namely:

- Reducing the management overhead cost (in principle the organizational overhead should go down as risk maturity grows)
- Increasing efficiency (that is the way things are done)
- Exploiting knowledge
- Leveraging opportunities within the organization.

The idea that risk imposes costs on an organization is central to much of the practical application within risk management. A prime aim of continuous improvement therefore must be to reduce the cost burden on the organization. If such cost can be identified then the impact of risk on the organization can be measured (see also discussion on risk metrics), and decisions to reduce poor performance in the management of risk can be made in a rational way. This can be achieved by comparing the cost of such performance against the benefits couched in terms of reductions in the cost of risk over time. A continuous improvement risk plan by itself lacks context and purpose. It is therefore essential that the continuous improvement risk plan is not only developed in line with the risk management framework (discussed in previous chapters) but that it is maintained in harmony with the framework throughout its life cycle. See Figure 4.2 for clarification.

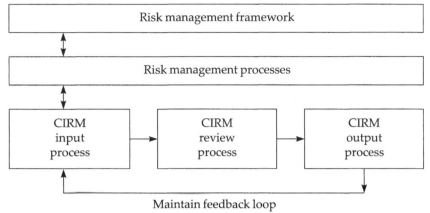

Figure 4.2
Continuous improvement
risk model (CIRM)

Clearly the achievability of any continuous improvement programme is constrained by its affordability and although there are many elements that determine the achievability of the programme it is the costing of these elements that establishes the organization's affordability benchmark. Typical elements will include both fixed and variable costs. For example:

- Staff resources
- Documentation (modification and reviews)
- Training and presentations (including communication)
- Additional software
- System updating
- Expansion and development
- Ongoing configuration and release management.

4.3.3 Competent personnel trained in the use of risk management practices

Some aspects of training in risk management techniques and practices have already been explored in Chapters 2 and 3. In the context of the heading I would like to focus on the competency requirements which project managers and their team members need to manage the more complex aspects of software development project risk. In doing so I have drawn on material taken from the Association for Project Managers and the USA Project Management Institute, Body of Knowledge (BoK).

Subject matter	Subject details	Reference material
General Topics	Understanding what project risk management is. This includes the terminology of risk and what elements make up the risk management process. Defining what the benefits are and an understanding of the cultural aspects of risk management together with stakeholder analysis. The three main heuristics and their importance in risk management including roles and responsibilities: *Heuristics:* 1. Representativeness 2. Availability 3. Adjustment and anchoring	• PRAM • BoK (PMI) • BS 6079 (Part 3) • RAMP
Define project	The need for stakeholder analysis and the need for objectives analysis	• BS 6079 (Part 3) • PRAM
Focus risk management	Understanding the elements of the risk management plan and the different stages within the project life cycle	• PRAM
Risk identification	Understanding the techniques used in identifying risk	• PRAM
Risk assessment	Understanding the causes of risk, and how risk can be classified and the use of risk assessment statements and reports	• PRAM
Qualitative risk assessment	Understanding how qualitative techniques can be used and applied to prioritize risk	• PRAM
Quantitative risk assessment	Understanding how quantitative techniques can be used and applied to prioritize risk	
Risk treatment and planning	Understanding the need for risk response strategies and how such strategies can be developed including contingency plans	• PRAM
Risk management	Understanding the need for monitoring risk including the development of risk registers. Why senior management and stakeholder buy-in are crucial. The importance of people and the key factors involved in implementing risk management strategies. Personal attitudes to risk and their importance to risk management. The need for risk reporting and risk ownership together with undertaking risk reviews	• PRAM

Figure 4.3 Risk management competency profile

Figure 4.3 identifies the subject matter that practitioners in project management need to have knowledge of if they are to be considered competent in risk management. The codes specified in the reference column identify where information may be found.

4.3.4 Risk and software metrics

As previously discussed the responsibility for risk management at the project level clearly lies with the project manager who should be responsible for setting the strategy and implementing the risk strategy, although it is also clear that everyone within the team bears some risk management responsibility. This responsibility and accountability should be clearly set out in the project team's terms of reference.

There is an old management adage which says 'what gets measured gets managed'. Developing metrics for use in managing risk is perhaps one of the most neglected aspects of risk management and some would say one of the most difficult to implement. Yet without some form of measurement in place how do we truly know we have things under control?

4.3.4.1 Software metrics

For software development projects a number of metrics have been developed which the project manager can adopt. For example, it is generally accepted that poorly written requirements are a principal source of project risk. The metrics and attributes defined in Figure 4.4 are related to project risk. The metrics for ambiguity – the count of weak phrases and optional phrases in the requirements document – indicate problems in the requirements document that can result in confusion and the need to take unplanned actions to resolve the questions raised. In essence the higher the count of ambiguous terms, the higher the risk. Software metrics can be classified into two types according to whether they are predictive or prescriptive. For example, a prescriptive metric describes the state of the software at the time of measurement, for example a reliability metric might be based on the number of tested lines of code.

Requirement	Metric	Benchmark	Risk management
Ambiguity in requirements	Weak phrases examples include: • adequate • as a minimum • be able to • be capable of • but not limited to • provide for	No more than 10 weak phrases per 1000 requirements or 1%	• Trend analysis • Additional cost to rework document • Feedback to client

Figure 4.4 Example of software metrics

Criteria	Definition
Objectivity	The results should be free from subjective influences. It must not matter who the measurer is
Reliability	The results should be precise and repeatable
Validity	The metric must ensure the correct characteristic
Standardization	The metric must be unambiguous and allow for comparison
Comparability	The metric must be comparable with other measures of the same criterion
Economy	The simpler and, therefore, the cheaper the measure is to use the better
Usefulness	The measure must address a need, not simply measure a property for its own sake

Figure 4.5 Seven criteria for a good metric (after Watts 1987)

In answering the question what makes a good metric, I am drawn to the criteria developed by Watts (1987). He suggests seven criteria of goodness for a software metric. These are given in Figure 4.5. In the final analysis no matter what measures are used they must be consistent. It could be argued that no one metric is a precise risk determinant in the analysis of a software project. Whilst poor quality of any product is a risk to the specific objectives of a project, some of the better measures of risk come from correlations of basic metrics. Complexity of code and size of software modules under development are two examples where correlation allows us to assess risk against software industry benchmarks, see Figure 4.6.

4.4 Risk management tools

The expansion of the discipline of risk management in software projects has encouraged the development and favourable use of software tools in this area. Any risk management tool (and there are many to choose from, see Appendix B) should support where appropriate the organization's integrated project management processes aligned with the strategic goals and objectives.

The selection of a risk management tool should be undertaken on the basis of strategic use rather than tactical application because risk management tools are expensive if introduced at an enterprise level. Strategic choice is very much influenced by:

Category	Measure
Milestone performance	• Milestone dates
Work in progress (See Figure 4.7 for examples)	• Requirements • Components • Test cases • Problem reports • Changes
Schedule performance	• Schedule variance
Incremental capability	• Build content (component) • Build content (function)
Effort profile	• Effort
Staff profile	• Staff levels • Staff experience • Staff turnover
Cost performance	• Cost variance • Cost profile
Environment availability	• Resource availability • Resource utilization
Product size and stability	• Lines of code • Number of components • Words of memory • Database size
Functional size and stability	• Requirements • Function points
Target CPU	• CPU • I/O • Memory • Storage • Response times
Defect profile	• Problem trends • Problem ageing
Complexity	• Cyclomatic complexity
Process maturity	• BS 6079
Productivity	• Functional size/effort ratio • Product size/effort ratio
Rework	• Rework • Rework effort

Figure 4.6
Industry metrics by category

- Who will the likely users be?
- What role will the tool fulfil?
- What benefits can be expected, and for whom?
- What effect will the tool have on the management of risk in your operations?

In principle the type of features offered by commercial products tend to meet 70–80 per cent of the needs of most organizations.

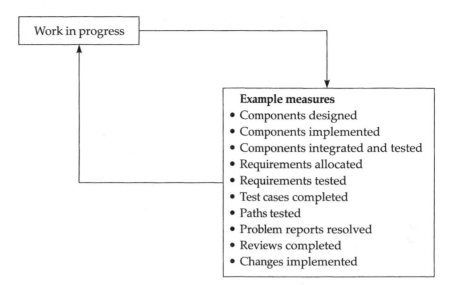

Figure 4.7
Example selecting
measures

Where features are not catered for, bespoke development may be the way forward but this can be an expensive option.

A review of the commercial risk management products in Appendix B, highlights an A–Z of generic risk management features and attributes to be taken into consideration when considering *which* risk management tool. Those identified include:

- Analysis and assessment by risk type
- Breakdown structures at project level
- Costs (by risk type)
- Decision support (drill down by risk type and cluster)
- Exposure matrix
- Generic risk classification
- Influence diagrams (and maps)
- Modelling
- Metrics
- Plans (mitigation and contingency planning by risk type)
- Probability distribution matrix
- Qualitative analysis
- Quantitative analysis
- Ranking
- Reports (including graphic distributions)
- Simulation (Monte Carlo and what if scenarios).

4.4.1 Expert tools in risk management

In global software development a small number of organizations have turned their attention to developing risk applications which incorporate the ethos of risk expert systems (RES). Such systems are growing in popularity and are seen as problem-solving tools for complex risk management situations. One reason why software organizations are turning to RES is cost and availability of good domain experts and RES are seen as a means of mitigation and future knowledge sharing.

Clearly the development of RES for risk management is different from that of standard software packages (although some features are inherent). The key to developing such systems is deciding what knowledge should be encoded into the system.

The term 'expert system' is derived from work in the science of artificial intelligence. In essence expert systems are computer programs that are designed to mimic the working of a human expert. Expert systems in risk management address problems normally thought to require domain expertise for their solution. Performance requirements for RES are the ability to perform at a level of an expert, using the knowledge of human experts, whilst matching the results of a competent human expert. RES should be designed to raise the level of expertise, by augmenting the individual's reasoning process or capability in a particular domain. Expert systems in risk management must be able to explain their reasoning or justify their decisions on demand in a manner that is intelligible by the user. In short, RES should be thought of as a model of the expertise of best practitioners in the field.

Developing a RES first involves extracting the relevant knowledge from the human expert. Such knowledge is often heuristic in nature, based on useful 'rules of thumb' rather than absolute certainties. Extracting it from the expert in a way that can be used by a computer is generally a difficult task, requiring its own expertise. Usually a knowledge engineer has the job of extracting this knowledge and building the expert system knowledge base.

4.4.1.1 RES methodology

RES generally involve a great deal of time and money and for those contemplating the development of RES there are a number of requirements to address:

- Setting the objectives
- Knowledge acquisition
- Knowledge representation

- System testing
- System validation.

To avoid costly and embarrassing failures, sets of guidelines to determine whether a problem is suitable for a RES solution have been developed. They are:

1 The need for a solution must justify the costs involved in development. There must be a realistic assessment of the costs and benefits involved.
2 Human expertise is not available in all situations where it is needed. If the 'expert' knowledge is widely available it is unlikely that it will be worth developing an expert system. However, in areas like business re-engineering there may be rare specialized knowledge which could be cheaply provided by an expert system, as and when required, without having to fly in your friendly (but very highly paid) expert.
3 The problem may be solved using symbolic reasoning techniques. It shouldn't require manual dexterity or physical skill.
4 The problem is well structured and does not require (much) common sense knowledge. Common sense knowledge is notoriously hard to capture and represent. It turns out that highly technical fields are easier to deal with, and tend to involve relatively small amounts of well-formalized knowledge.
5 The problem cannot be easily solved using more traditional computing methods. If there's a good algorithmic solution to a problem, you don't want to use an expert system.
6 Co-operative and articulate experts exist. For an expert system project to be successful it is essential that the experts are willing to help, and don't feel that their job is threatened! You also need any management and potential users to be involved and have positive attitudes to the whole thing.
7 The problem is of proper size and scope. Typically you need problems that require highly specialized expertise, but would only take a human expert a short time to solve (say an hour at most).

It should be clear that only a small range of problems might be appropriate for RES technology. However, given a suitable problem, RES can bring enormous benefits. Systems have been developed, for example, to help configure computer systems and reduce failures in testing software.

4.4.1.2 RES benefits

Organizations that have persevered and introduced RES have reported the following benefits:

- Offer greater speed in coming to a decision, easier access to expertise and greater reliability and consistency
- Aid consistency, reliability and record keeping
- Impart good practice to the user
- Sharpen up the available human expertise
- Improve ability to communicate complex and judgemental expertise.

In addition to the direct benefits of RES, there are a number of indirect benefits that have been reported, namely:

- The actual process of knowledge elicitation can help sharpen an expert's thinking, by forcing him/her to reconsider the rules s/he uses and order in which s/he works
- The process of extracting and codifying scattered or dis-organized knowledge can reveal that certain key facts are missing, or uncover new, previously unrealized facts
- Since human expertise is both fragile and transient the ability to archive the expert's knowledge improves its accessibility.

(Sangster)

4.5 Risk mitigation strategies

In Chapter 1 we discussed the project environment and how the environment was comprised of many variables including the market, cultural diversity, stakeholders, economic and legal entities. We also discussed the essence of organizational policy and how such policies are a reflection of the organization's culture. Attitude to risk is often mirrored by the policy decisions taken by senior management. Risk management and mitigation strategies may already exist that define the amount of risk management to be done, irrespective of the project environment. Conversely, there may be an existing approach to risk mitigation that leads to tailoring, depending on further analysis, to a specific project. Some organizations make it easier to implement risk mitigation strategies than others, depending on their risk awareness and level of risk maturity.

In software projects consideration needs to be given to both macro and micro risks. The existence of both risk types will affect the scope of risk mitigation. For example, more time and effort will be required if the project is to be implemented in an unstable client environment using new technology.

Experience would suggest that organizations tend to adopt one of four strategies when developing plans for risk mitigation. These are:

1 Avoidance strategies (generic strategy eliminate uncertainty)
2 Transfer strategies (generic strategy allocate ownership)
3 Reduction strategies (generic strategy modify exposure)
4 Retention strategies (generic strategy include in baseline).

4.5.1 Avoidance strategies

In Chapter 1 (refer to point 1.8) we discussed the mood within the business world to move to litigation at the blink of an eye. For this reason risk avoidance is a critical element in today's litigious society. The term 'risk avoidance' can be described as 'changing project objectives, methods or activities to avoid the possibility of the risk occurring'.

In developing risk avoidance strategies the organization must weigh the potential value of the activity against the potential loss. Why? Risk avoidance strategies are expensive and can severely restrict a company's ability to conduct its business. As an example, take system security, where breaches in software security can cost projects and organizations millions of pounds. The following point was noted in a recent edition of CIO:

> *Attorneys say the following scenarios are likely to result in lawsuits, which may not be covered by normal business insurance. A Company's best defence will be proof that it follows security best practices – from establishing an in-house security policy to testing how well those procedures actually work.*

- *Breach of contract (e.g. broken confidentiality)*
- *Denial-of-service attacks*
- *Received malicious code*
- *Personal injury (laws invoked from improper disclosure)*
- *Inappropriate web content (defacements)*
- *Not protecting shareholder value*

Taking this theme further in risk avoidance, IT organizations will usually try to think of everything that could go wrong and deploy every conceivable security measure 'just in case'. The execution is usually limited in terms of expenditure on security features and the need to balance it with business needs. In the absence of any alternative, arresting the prosecution of a risk avoidance strategy in mid-stream may well leave a company unknowingly and gravely exposed. The *raison d'être* of a risk avoidance strategy is to apply all possible safeguards; there is therefore no requirement to apply the most effective safeguards first. Thus, in the extreme case, by the time the security budget is cut, only the least effective safeguards will have been applied. The alternative is to build a 'castle' with just the right defensive strength for the business needs today, but with the ability to increase or relax that strength as the need arises. Key to the success of this alternate strategy is the ability to measure risk.

In practice there are two types of safeguard: threat safeguards and vulnerability safeguards. Threat safeguards reduce the ability of a threat to exploit vulnerability. Examples are physical barriers (which reduce physical access) and firewalls (which reduce electronic access). Vulnerability safeguards will either eradicate the vulnerability totally, or limit the damage that would result if it were exploited. Of these two types of safeguard, the threat safeguard has the most dramatic effects, as it will reduce the risk due to *all* vulnerabilities that could be exploited by that threat. In contrast the vulnerability safeguard only mitigates the risk due to individual vulnerabilities (Brewer 1999).

4.5.2 Transfer strategies

As previously suggested project risks are not of equal importance and risks tend to be interrelated with a lot of overlap existing between categories. For example, the risk of lack of skilled J2EE developers with new web-based portal technology involves three classifications. The first organization risk is the lack of experienced programmers, which illustrates the organization's inability to support the project. Second, a project risk, as the lack of experienced personnel or the contracting-in of experienced individuals raises the risks inherent in the project. Finally, there is the technical risk associated with the use of new technology relative to the project.

The aim of transfer strategies is to identify another stakeholder better able to manage the risk, to which the liability and responsibility for action can be passed. So if the shortage of skilled J2EE programmers were identified as a key risk we may consider a risk transfer strategy that allows us to utilize any technology partnership arrangements that might be in place or labour from other client projects. Alternatively offshore development or the use of contract or software agencies may be appropriate. We must, however, be careful in our decision making in that we do not swap one risk for another.

A number of contractual mechanisms can be used to transfer risk between different stakeholders. For example, risk reward arrangements are becoming more popular with organizations that wish to transfer risk to third parties. It is important that in developing a risk transfer strategy that it does not become abdication of responsibility on the part of the project manager, who should retain an active involvement in the management of all risks that could affect its delivery.

Contractual mechanisms, however, carry their own risks. These risks include:

- Client problems
- Delays
- Events, such as *force majeure*
- Insurance and indemnities
- Joint venture relationships.

Risk transfer tactics include some dos and don'ts:

- Do periodical audit contracts
- Do use additional insured status to back up indemnity agreements
- Do seek endorsements
- Do deal proactively with problems
- Do develop a strategy for risk transfer
- Do negotiate for reasonable requirements
- Do use a blanket endorsement to reduce the chances of breach
- Do consider your contractual obligations when you choose your limits
- Don't use overly restricted requirements
- Don't use an unenforceable indemnity agreement
- Don't rely solely on an indemnity agreement
- Don't agree to provide reciprocal or mutual status
- Don't require the other party to endorse its policy to be primary and non-contributory
- Don't put too much faith in certificates (of any kind)
- Don't simply accept requirements as offered
- Don't forget your limits are diluted every time you sign a contract.

The risk assessment process can provide the initial guide as to which party is best able to manage risks and the most appropriate form of contract. This information comes from identifying how risks might arise. The analysis also identifies the potential impacts, and so may aid in determining a fair price for taking the risks involved. Most risk transfer strategies require decisions to be taken very early in the life of a project, almost certainly in the pre-tender phases.

4.5.3 Reduction strategies

Risk reduction strategies are concerned with reducing the size of risk in order to make it more acceptable to the project or organization, by reducing the probability and/or the impact. Risks that fall into this category tend to be those that will have the greatest impact on the project and fall into the category of catastrophic and critical. As mentioned in Chapter 2, different mitigating measures can provide different levels of risk protection. For example, Figure 4.8 provides a risk mitigation strategy for those *legal risks* associated with software projects.

4.5.4 Retention strategies

Risk retention strategies recognize that residual risks must be taken, and responding either actively by allocating appropriate contingency, or passively doing nothing except monitoring the status of the risk.

In point 3.5.4 we discussed how a priority listing of risks provides a basis to set cut-off points to determine which risks may be discarded (minor) or identified as major and considered further. It was suggested that low level risks could simply be documented and accepted. As a working definition: low risks can be accepted given normal monitoring and control measures. Although we will discuss the monitoring of risks in more detail in Chapter 5, with risk retention strategies monitoring risks plays a crucial role.

Monitoring is appropriate where the remaining risk levels are insufficient to justify potential treatment options or where it is not possible or is uneconomic to treat the residual risk. It is not possible or cost effective to eliminate all risk attached to software projects.

Selecting the best strategy involves trade-offs between the potential benefits of implementing a retention strategy and the

Project XYZ legal matters identified

Intellectual property rights, Data Protection Act, data security, data management, future Acts of Parliament, disputes management, contract management, prosecutions, bankruptcy and contract staff.

Action to be taken	Whom
1 Restrict material to known copyright owners who have assigned copyright for project	Legal advisor
2 Manage data integrity by ensuring secure access to massed data, stored media and appropriate passwords and permissions	Data architect
3 Meet any standards set as part of IPR agreements	Project manager
4 Ensure reviews of documentation	Project manager
5 Deploy legally verified disclaimers on documentation	Legal advisor
6 Prevent release of information relating to storage locations being released (physical/electronic)	Project manager
7 Appoint external arbiter to preside over disputes	Account manager
8 Ensure contract procedures, content and management are agreed by legal department and are managed according to the contract	Legal advisor
9 Use established companies with good reference and appropriate financial clearances checked before doing business	Account manager
10 Retain transition plan for alternative contractor	Project manager
11 Share contracted staff with other organizations	Project manager
12 Ensure legal, insurance, and employment contracts appropriately in place for project staff	Project manager
13 Refer legal matters immediately	Project manager

Figure 4.8
Strategy for reducing project risks

actual costs of managing it. Established practice may assist in selecting alternatives but the overall objective is to recognize which risks to address and which risks to accept, and to confidently select the best value response.

As part of this process, it is useful to examine risks at the project or programme level in order to develop wider decision rules for controlling and managing risk at a strategic level. The aim is to identify common risks and general responses that occur in more than one circumstance or that have wide potential effects.

4.6 Formulating and implementing risk management plans

In the previous section we discussed the four options to consider when planning for risks, that is avoidance, transfer, reduction and retention strategies. Project complexity is often seen as a function of the technology, schedule and resource intensity parameters. All of these factors should be assessed as part of the four options. A fast-track project schedule with little room for flexibility increases the scope of risk planning, as does a project with scarce resources. Equally, a project that will implement new or complex technology increases the amount of risk planning.

Risk planning can be described as *the function of deciding what if anything should be done about risk or a set of related risks*. In this function decisions and mitigation strategies are developed based on current knowledge of project risks.

4.6.1 Why create a risk plan?

A risk management plan is a helpful formal way to report on designated or major undertakings. It should summarize the results of the risk management process, action strategies and implementation framework. In particular, it should also describe the risk management measures to be implemented to reduce and control risks. For major risks risk action schedules should be prepared to assign individual responsibilities and timeframes and identify those who are responsible for follow-up.

In formulating risk plans a number of key rules should be adhered to, they include:

- Early agreement on risk requirements
- Commitment and involvement of the project manager and user community
- Attention and decisions by the project board
- A core set of definitions and measures on risk
- Documenting decisions.

Documenting the decisions is essential. For example, as you record, gaps appear and inconsistencies protrude. Creating the risk plan usually requires lots of mini-decisions and these can bring clarity to the project.

The risk plan communicates the decisions to others. Often what we assume is common knowledge is unknown by other members of the project team. Fundamentally, the project manager's goal is to keep everyone progressing in the same direction and communication is essential to achieve this goal. The risk plan makes communicating a lot easier.

The risk plan is a wealth of information as well as a checklist. By reviewing the risk plan, as often as is required, the project manager knows what corrective action or changes of emphasis or shifts in direction are needed.

It is a fact that 80 per cent of a project manager's time should be spent on communication: hearing, reporting, and counselling. The other 20 per cent is spent on activities where the project manager needs information that is data based. The risk plan and risk statements are a critical set of documents that should meet this need.

The job of the project manager is to develop a risk plan and to manage it. The risk plan consists of documents on who, what, why, when, where, how and how much. The plan encapsulates much of the project manager's work. If their comprehensive and critical nature is recognized in the beginning, the manager can approach them as friendly tools rather than an annoying overhead. The project manager can set the direction much more quickly by doing so.

4.6.2 Key steps in formulating the risk plans

1 Specify the risk management plan for identifying, analysing, and prioritizing project risk factors (see Figure 4.9)
2 Specify plans for assessing initial risk factors and for the ongoing identification, assessment, and mitigation of risk factors throughout the life cycle of the project
3 Describe the following:

- procedures for contingency planning
- procedures for tracking the various risk factors
- procedures for evaluating changes in the levels of the risk factors and responding to changes in the levels of the risk factors
- risk management work activities
- procedures and schedules for performing risk management work activities
- risk documentation and reporting requirements
- organizations and personnel responsible for performing specific risk management activities

- procedures for communicating risks and risk status amongst the various customer, project and subcontractor organizations.

4 Identify and describe the applicable impact of any of the following risk factors:

- risks in the customer–project relationship
- contractual risks
- technological risks
- risks caused by the size and complexity of the product
- risks in the development and target environments
- risks in personnel acquisition, skill levels and retention
- risks to schedule and budget
- risks in achieving customer acceptance of the deliverables.

4.6.3 Product breakdown structure (PBS)

The use of PBS methods in risk planning is becoming more commonplace in software projects largely due to the adoption of PRINCE2 (Projects in a Controlled Environment). The process involves the product-based planning technique to ensure plans are based on required outputs:

- Create a PBS which identifies the products required
- Write product descriptions which include defining the quality requirements for each product
- Produce a product flow diagram which shows the logical order of creation of the products and their interdependencies
- Identify activities required to create the products
- Estimate duration and effort for each activity
- Assess risks
- Calculate costs
- Identify management points needed
- Document the plan, its assumptions and supporting text.

The benefit of using PBS is that it does help identify in a structured form all elements of the project and provides a comprehensive framework for assessing each and every aspect of the project deliverables for potential risks. The PBS also provides a direct description of the system hierarchy and interfaces for the purpose of identifying risk propagation.

PBS in software projects tends to be linked to work packages – PBS provides a single point of ownership (or contact) for each risk through the management structure, that is the person responsible for delivering the work package.

Heading	Suggested content
Summary	Describe what's in the document emphasis on how risks will be managed including risk management structure
Risk background	Description of risk Source of risk Risk indicator
Risk assessment	Summary of risk impact Ranking of risks Risk propagation Impact on time and cost
Risk ownership	Who will own the risk (for example, organization, project, or third party)
Risk approach	Risk objectives Risk methodology to be adopted Risk measures Risk budget Critical success factors Alternative approaches and contingency plans Agenda points Decision points and actions
Key inputs	Reference documents Risk statements Risk chronology Risk closure statements

Figure 4.9
Template for risk management plan

4.6.4 Costing the plan

Affordability is the key here. Although there are many elements that determine the achievability of the risk plan it is the costing of these elements that establishes the benchmark implementation plan. Getting the costing of the risk management process correct is essential for two reasons:

1 When combined with the costs from the risk response plan, project risk can be quantified in terms meaningful to decision makers. It is the combined costs and risk-planning costs that experienced senior managers will use as the basis to formulate a business decision to either proceed with or cancel the project.

2 Accurate costing of the risk plan should lead to an accurate risk-planning budget, which if approved, provides the necessary funding to develop and maintain the risk management process throughout the project life cycle. If improperly or inaccurately costed, the risk plan will be ineffective in

119

developing the structure necessary to adequately manage project risk, thereby consigning the entire project to a higher risk state.

(De Bakker, Stewart and Shermeta 2002)

4.6.5 Implementing the risk management plan

In Chapter 2 we discussed the key aspects of communication and structured walkthroughs – having gone through the process of preparing the risk management plan the next activity is to implement it. At this point it is important to get the communication channels working and the various stakeholders on board to sell the plan.

It is generally accepted good practice to send out the risk plan for review prior to issuing it as a configuration document. Typically, the risk plan is distributed to function, domain and third party managers who are responsible for risk in their specific areas. Occasionally it may be prudent to share the risk plan with customers especially where dependencies are acknowledged as important critical success factors.

Consensus seems to be that the review format described in Chapter 2 works. It is an effective method for managing risks and creating a common understanding of risks by all individuals who have some ownership in the project. The review and implementation process also promotes a disciplined approach to handling sensitive issues.

When implementing the risk plan it is vital to remember that such plans are not entirely people centred. Risk plans will incorporate such artefacts as the policies, procedures and political statements (sometimes with disregard to who does what).

All projects (even good ones, as I can testify) will experience some degree of failure simply because of cause-and-effect behaviours. Realistically we sometimes just have to get on and cope with the situation and revise our thinking and plans accordingly, and hope senior management will support you.

4.7 Self-assessment checklist

Ask yourself	Yes	No	Not sure
Risk planning			
• Have standards for risk planning been introduced?	☐	☐	☐
• If so, has the project manager initiated the use of risk planning on the project?	☐	☐	☐
• If so, have risk-planning sessions been organized?	☐	☐	☐
• If so, has a facilitator been appointed?	☐	☐	☐
• Has the project manager established both strategic and tactical objectives for risk planning?	☐	☐	☐
• If so, have short, medium, and long term goals been established?	☐	☐	☐
• Has the project manager identified risk reduction options for discussion?	☐	☐	☐
• Have these options been discussed with immediate members of the project team?	☐	☐	☐
• If so, have these options been evaluated?	☐	☐	☐
• Have these options been discussed with other key stakeholders?	☐	☐	☐
• Has the project manager and the project team demonstrated adherence to risk standards in planning?	☐	☐	☐
• Has provision been made to transfer knowledge gained during the risk planning sessions back into the company risk management process?	☐	☐	☐
Risk management tools			
• Has the company invested in risk management tools?	☐	☐	☐
• If so, does the project manager have access to these risk management tools?	☐	☐	☐
• If so, are these tools being used within the risk planning process?	☐	☐	☐
• If so, are these tools being used to generate management information on risk?	☐	☐	☐
• If so, is there scope to introduce RES based tools?	☐	☐	☐
Risk mitigation and implementation			
• Has the project manager defined the scope of risk mitigation for the project?	☐	☐	☐
• If so, does it embrace one or more of the four generic strategies: avoidance, transfer, reduction and/or retention?	☐	☐	☐
• If so, has the project manager agreed the appropriate strategy with all risk owners and key stakeholders?	☐	☐	☐
• Has the project manager prepared a risk management plan?	☐	☐	☐
• If so, has this plan been communicated to all risk owners and key stakeholders?	☐	☐	☐
• Has the project manager adhered to the five key rules?	☐	☐	☐
• Has the project manager established a change control and feedback process?	☐	☐	☐
• If so, is this process known and understood by everyone?	☐	☐	☐

| 5 | Monitoring risk in software development projects |

5.1 Recap on Chapter 4

From the previous chapter you will have ascertained how important it is to understand the necessity for risk mitigation planning, setting objectives and their associated goals.

In the previous chapter we also looked at risk from the context of best practice and discussed the need for properly defined standards. We also reviewed those standards common to software projects in risk management.

We discussed the need for continuous improvement in risk management and its link to risk cost reduction. We also revisited the application of software risk metrics to projects including the development of such metrics for projects. We also explored risk management tools especially the use of risk expert systems. Finally, we explored risk mitigation and the use of the four strategies (avoidance, transfer, reduction and retention) and how such strategies could be employed within the context of software projects and their application and input to the construction of risk plans.

In this chapter we will explore the process for monitoring risk. We will also discuss the use of risk support systems and the formulation of risk registers, and the mechanisms used to track risk. We will also debate the use of reporting tools and look at some aspects of negotiation in risk management.

5.2 Developing a process for monitoring risk

The frequency of monitoring and the responsibility for it should be specified in the risk management plan. Monitoring of risks and risk management effectiveness should be a routine and recognized activity and part of the risk management framework (see Figure 5.1). Monitoring risk is critical because the one risk attribute whose influence is difficult to predict is 'time'. Generalizations about risk made early in the project can (and often do) decay with time. One reason for performing risk monitoring is to keep a predictable, unpredictable, or unknown risk from becoming a known one. Monitoring occurs after the decisions about mitigation strategies and tactics have been implemented to:

- Check if the consequences of our decisions are the same as envisioned
- Identify opportunities for refinement in the area of risk mitigation
- Help provide feedback for future decisions about controlling those new or current risks not responding to risk mitigation or whose nature has changed with time.

In developing a process for monitoring risks we should consider a number of key requirements and although some have been previously stated I believe it is worthwhile spelling them out again. They are:

- The number of people available to undertake the task of risk monitoring/management

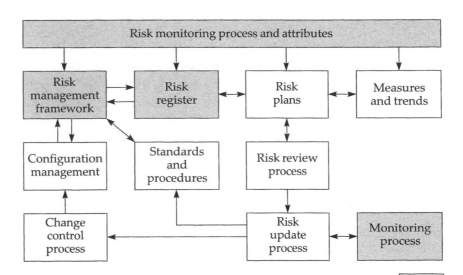

Figure 5.1
Risk monitoring

- The likely extent of preparatory work required for commencing this activity
- The likely range of issues that need exploring
- The extent to which a participatory approach to the task is envisaged (this will increase the time required significantly). Experience suggests that more time is often needed to fully involve stakeholders or beneficiaries in the project preparation process than in some cases has been allowed
- The number of third parties involved in the project or activity which will need to be visited
- The number of different locations that the project team or individuals in the team will have to visit (for example, if offshore development is being used)
- The remoteness of location assignments needing extensive consultation will require significantly expanded time
- The extent to which extensive preliminary or wrap-up activities or meetings are required
- The likely time requirements for writing reports, and the expected size of reports, number of essential documents, etc.
- The number of people who are likely to need to comment on the reports and the extent of their involvement.

5.2.1 Safeguards

In setting up the risk monitoring process care should be taken to ensure that there is adequate separation of duties in key elements of the risk management process to avoid potential conflicts of interest. The project manager should ensure that sufficient safeguards exist to minimize the potential that individuals initiating risk-taking positions may inappropriately influence key control functions of the risk management process such as the development and enforcement of policies and procedures (Figure 5.1) and the reporting of risks to senior management. The nature and scope of such safeguards should be in accordance with the size and structure of the project. They should also be commensurate with the complexity of risk incurred by the project and the complexity of its commitments. Larger or more complex projects should have a designated risk manager responsible for the design and administration of the projects' risk measurement, monitoring and control functions. The control functions carried out by this person, such as administering the risk limits, should be part of the overall internal control system.

5.2.2 Verification

The personnel charged with monitoring and controlling risk should have a well-founded understanding of all types of software risk faced throughout the project and during the project risk monitoring cycle. The following verification activities are considered necessary activities for the management team to mitigate project risk:

- Review periodic reports of the project team and/or project manager, to ensure that the project continues to meet business needs
- Provide information as needed by the project, and authorize the work to proceed if the project is meeting plans and commitments
- Participate in formal project reviews, reviewing status and handling action items
- Review the business case (or cost–benefit analysis, as appropriate) on a regular basis, to ensure that this project should continue
- Review activities of the project team on an ongoing basis, to verify that they are following their plan and the relevant processes of the organization
- Review the results of work product reviews and testing, to ensure that the project deliverables meet customer requirements and project quality plans
- Review change management and configuration management activities, to ensure they follow the organization processes and that baselines are under control.

5.2.3 Monitoring of third party risk

Some software projects are undertaken as joint ventures or on a risk reward basis. In such situations it is not uncommon for such third parties to own and be responsible for monitoring their specific risks. For example, where subcontractors are considered critical to the delivery process, the project manager must ensure that risk controls are in place and that the governing organization or project board has formally approved such controls. This provides a mechanism for bounding the project organization's responsibility. A word of advice here, even when a third party owns a risk, and is managing it, the project organization should still consider the need for additional mitigation within the risk plan.

5.2.4 Key deliverables

The monitoring and controlling of risks will generate a number of key deliverables, these include:

- Written status (or PRINCE highlight) reports
- Updates to lists of action items, risks, problems, and issues
- Updates to the plan and schedule, to reflect actual progress
- Comparisons of actual costs to budgeted costs, as well as the cost–benefit analysis used when starting the project
- Audit and review reports of the activities and work products under development

5.2.5 Macro risk indicators

Research on software risk would suggest that efforts to strengthen software project risk analysis described by some projects typically involve more careful monitoring of a set of macro indicators and the quicker adjustment of exposures. These indicators include variables such as time, cost, and quality. If critical values of the indicator variables for a project are exceeded, the project manager can initiate reviews of a project's risk rating, contingency limits and warranty requirements. This indicating regime could be applied to your highly visible risks, that is the top 10 or 15 risks.

Interestingly when projects are in crisis, project managers tend to strengthen the monitoring process in an effort to identify problems and to adjust exposure in a prompt and more systematic manner in response to measured changes in risk. The monitoring of risk tends to become more micro focused rather than being done on a wider project basis. On balance, it could be argued that this strategy is perfectly feasible but experience would suggest that gaps tend to emerge when risk is not integrated into the wider project process, especially at the programme level.

5.3 Formulating a project risk database/risk register

The project risk register (PRR) is a key attribute of the risk monitoring process and is described as the formal record of identified risks. A body of information listing all risks identified for the project, explaining the nature of each risk and recording information relevant to its assessment and management.

In essence the PRR is a chronology of a risk's life history. As portrayed in Figure 5.1 the PRR is a document that should be kept under strict configuration management. The PRR should contain all of the important risks, as it reflects the lack of knowledge at the start of the project, and the gradual resolution of those uncertainties. Experience would suggest that the PRR has two main functions. The first is a body of knowledge that all team members have access to, this is certainly required for major projects to enable key risk owners to make and record their decisions. Often software engineers involved in one aspect of the development process have a surprisingly unclear view of the issues involved in other aspects, and many of the problems in software projects stem from the interfaces between aspects, rather than problems within them. This is certainly the case in projects where multiple suppliers are used or in consortia-based projects. In such situations a formal repository of risk knowledge is useful, indeed the project manager should become one of the people on the project with a good overview. With respect to consortia projects the PRR must be seen as having been developed in an unbiased way, either because the project manager is independent, or because the management board with representation from the consortia censuses the risk data.

The second main function of the PRR is to initiate the plans that flow from it. Figure 5.1 shows this flow. It starts with the risk register; this provides the data for time, cost and quality analyses. It also provides the foundation for the risk management plan, and it assists in the making of decisions on which risks the project should retain.

The use of the PRR as a decision-making tool means that these three aspects are not assumed to be independent, although it still enables separate analyses to be carried out. As a point of interest, integrated analysis, however, is usually required when the risk owners have the freedom to set some of the project parameters.

Remember that the integrated risk management process will fail if the risk register is not maintained. Preventative strategies include:

1 Project board to nominate an appropriate project manager to maintain the register throughout the project life cycle
2 Internal audit to monitor and report on maintenance of the integrated risk management register.

5.3.1 The risk database (and register)

Databases are one of the most effective ways to document risks, particularly when they are linked to other project information such as problems and issues, schedules, and change control. Databases are also a repository for collecting statistics on projects and adding to the body of knowledge on risk management.

If you choose not to procure a proprietary risk database product you could use a product such as Microsoft Access. To develop your own risk database (or register) the following attributes are considered appropriate:

- Project name: the project the risk is being reported under.
- Risk identifier: person responsible for identifying the risk.
- Date opened: the date the risk form was first filled out.
- Updated: this is the date the record was last edited. It should be filled out every time a change is made.
- Date closed: the date the risk report was closed.
- Risk ID: this field is automatically assigned, and cannot be changed by the user.
- Risk mitigator: this is the person assigned to mitigate the risk. If any questions arise about the risk, this is the one who should be contacted.
- Risk name: name given to the risk.
- Priority: the importance rank, from 1 to 5, based on the priority matrix.
- Status: indicates the current status of the risk.
- Life cycle: the type of life cycle being used on the project, such as waterfall and spiral.
- Life cycle stage: once the life cycle has been chosen, the appropriate stage can be chosen.
- Closure criteria: this is a checkpoint to make sure the risk was really eliminated, and that the mitigation decided upon was followed.
- Mitigation: these are the steps taken to combat/reduce the risk.
- Metrics: this information measures where the project is and where it is going. One example of this is how many risks of type X exist and how they are being addressed.
- Additional comments: this field should contain information relevant to the risk but not covered in any of the previous fields.

Again if you choose not to use Microsoft Access the construction of a simple risk register can be developed using other Microsoft Office products such as Excel or Word. The key attributes of a risk register include:

- Project name
- Risk identification number
- Description of risk
- Likelihood of risk occurring (score)
- Severity or impact (score)
- Overall risk (score)
- Risk strategy (for example, retain)
- Responsibility for risk
- Control procedure (actions)
- Monitoring process
- Potential cost (opportunity cost)
- Review date.

5.3.2 Benefits

Whether you use complex or simple tools, this formalized risk registration process has a number of advantages:

1 It enables the time, cost, and technical risk analyses and the risk reduction and risk transfer planning to be undertaken and carried out, and a configuration controlled document to be created and maintained throughout the project life cycle.
2 It provides a central repository of knowledge around which risk management can be built.
3 It forms the basis of the required outputs from risk work, namely the risk analysis paper, the risk management plan and the risk mitigation plan.
4 It provides an audit trail, so that decisions made can be traced back to the assumptions, judgements and calculations on which they were based.
5 Finally, it forms an important interface with subsequent phases of the project, which take up the risk management plan.

5.3.3 Key roles

Although organization structures differ from company to company for medium to large-scale software projects there are generally four main actors within the process of generating and maintaining the risk register. These are:

1 The risk originator
2 The project manager
3 The project board (sometimes called the review group)
4 The project team.

5.3.3.1 The risk originator (or owner)

The risk originator initially identifies the risk and formally communicates the risk to the project manager. The risk originator is formally responsible for:

- The early identification of the risk within the project
- The formal documentation of the risk, through the completion of a risk statement
- The submission of the risk statement to the project manager for review.

5.3.3.2 Project manager

The project manager receives records and monitors the progress of all risks within a project. The project manager is formally responsible for:

- Receiving all risk statements and identifying which of the risks raised are appropriate to the project
- Recording all risks in the risk register
- Presenting all risks to the project board
- Reporting and communicating all decisions made by the project board
- Monitoring the progress of all risk mitigating actions assigned.

5.3.3.3 Project board

The project board will confirm the risk 'likelihood' and 'impact' and assign risk-mitigating actions where appropriate. The project board is formally responsible for:
- The regular review of all risks recorded in the risk register
- The identification of change requests required in order to mitigate risks raised
- The allocation of risk mitigating actions
- The closure of risks which have no outstanding actions and are no longer likely to impact the project.

5.3.3.4 Project team

The project team undertakes all risk mitigating actions delegated by the project board. Figure 5.2 illustrates the flow of data within the system.

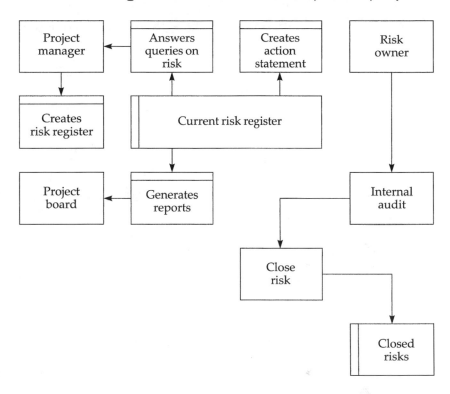

Figure 5.2
Risk register process
and data flow diagram

5.3.4 Responsibility

In principle once a risk has been assigned to someone, then only that person should have the authority to update the risk register information (although this activity is sometimes delegated to the project office). Generally speaking, the risk register for any risk can be accessed by whomever is assigned to the risk. However, the person responsible for a risk should provide routine status reports to the project manager for the weekly or monthly project review meetings (see also The project office, 5.4.1). The status for each risk should be reported on although typically only the top risks are discussed in detail. The risk register is used to report summary status information for risks.

5.4 Managing and tracking risk

An important function in the monitoring cycle is keeping track of those risks that pose the greatest threat. Tracking involves identification of your project's highest risk issues and tracking progress towards resolving those issues through subsequent progress reports. The major risk management benefits are similar to those of time, cost, and quality tracking plus the added ones of identifying and maintaining a high level risk consciousness.

As previously stated the most effective way to track risk is measurement. The significant risk reducing benefits achieved through a comprehensive measurement programme cannot be overstressed, although the use of software metrics does not, by itself, guarantee success in reducing risk. In the final analysis the use of metrics is an integral component of sound project management, which provides management with a benchmark for measuring the size and complexity of a proposed software project, as well as an indicator of the levels of risk that a project may face. The point here is that metrics data provide the means to compare your risk elements with historical data, pinpoint risk drivers, and determine alternative risk reduction choices. You must aggressively track and control the risk drivers affecting your project.

Tracking involves using techniques such as product break structures, metrics, quality indicators, activity networks, and *earned-value* methods to determine and track project progress with respect to plans, schedules, and budgets. Tracking is important because potential schedule slippages, cost overruns, and performance shortfalls are identified early, and their impact on other interdependent system elements reduced. Other risk tracking methods are peer inspections, reviews, audits, and meetings. See Figure 5.3.

Method or tool	Use
Risk register	Used by everyone to document new risks and to add information as risks are managed.
Periodic review of project data	Used for routine or frequent identification of risks.
Metric for project metrics	Use project metrics to help identify and track risks.
Action statements lists	Used for developing a list of relatively simple mitigation actions.
Risk tracking spreadsheets	Used by project managers to succinctly report current status information about their teams' risks.
Selective tracking	Used by project managers to isolate the top 10–15 risks, which will get mitigation resources.

Figure 5.3
Tracking methods and tools

A point here about earned value – earned value provides a systematic approach for developing a work plan and executing, controlling, and measuring progress against the plan. It establishes realistic relationships amongst programme technical performance and associated schedules and budgets. It is useful in monitoring the effectiveness of risk handling actions in that it provides periodic comparisons of the actual work accomplished in terms of cost and schedule with the work planned and budgeted. As such, it provides a basis to determine if risk handling actions are achieving their targeted results

With selective tracking it is prudent to review at regular intervals the top 10 list as follows:

- How long has this risk been on the list?
- What rank was it last reviewed?
- What have we done to mitigate it in this period?
- What should its rank be this time?

As risks fall off the list due to reduced potential impact, elimination, or by turning into a problem, then the remaining list is examined for a new one to place in the top 10. This method focuses management's efforts on the risks with the most potential impact. The total number of identified risks determines whether 5, 10 or 15 risks are on the PRR.

5.4.1 The project office

Many software projects are tied to standards and procedures that must be adhered to throughout the project life. A project office (PO) is responsible for setting up procedural documentation and templates that will be used on the project. With consistent standards and procedures, better quality of information should be available about the project. This should allow the project manager to make better judgement calls on risk related issues.

In Chapter 1, Figure 1.6, it was suggested that the tracking of risk could be undertaken by the PO. On large and complex projects the function of tracking risk can be and usually is delegated to the PO.

In these circumstances the PO is normally accountable to one of three people, the programme manager, project manager or risk manager. The PO's remit is to ensure that the agreed mitigation actions are keeping the risks under control and to ensure that the monitoring process is effective and timely enough to deal with issues. Open communication is an important characteristic of managing risk – given this situation the PO needs to understand the boundaries within which it will operate.

It invariably takes time to establish open communication and for the PO to become comfortable discussing issues and concerns with senior managers. Experience would suggest that building up trust is a characteristic of the organization and project culture. People tend to worry about crises when they happen – project managers need to get the focus right.

On consortia projects it is not uncommon to have local risk co-ordinators (LRC). If this is the case these LRC should liaise with the PO over the details of their risk register. At a minimum they should provide information on significant changes to risks and any details on emerging risks. The PO will act as the communication channel for feedback on the implementation of the project risk management strategy and the risk processes that make up the strategy.

It is perhaps worth pointing out that all local risk and other documentation should be transferred to the PO and compilation of the project risk report is the main activity of the PO at this stage.

The benefit of using the PO is that an audit trail is automatically set up of all documents that are classified and placed in a database system from which key risk and lessons learnt can be abstracted in the project report.

5.4.2 Risk audits

Within project and software organizations the role of the auditors, particularly internal auditors; has started to change. Internal auditing is invited to take a more strategic role in risk assessment, risk management and risk prevention. Systems and concepts have been developed to expand the capabilities of internal auditors as the business and technical risk experts of the company.

Internal auditing is an independent, objective assurance and consulting activity designed to add value and improve an organization's operations. It helps an organization accomplish its objectives by bringing a systematic, disciplined approach to evaluate and improve the effectiveness of risk management, control, and governance processes. (Institute of Internal Auditing)

The project board should determine the scope and direction for auditing objectives for senior management and should be focused on assessing those areas representing the greatest risks to the project, for example at the project initiation stage. As discussed there are many approaches to risk analysis and management. Ideally, risk analysis will be performed as a risk management process within the organization – with or without direct involvement from internal auditing. Although not agreeable, if risk management is not a formal management process, then the risk auditor must assess risk and risk management and find ways to communicate with management to assure consistent views on risk.

Because risk assessment is an iterative process the results of risk assessments should be maintained in a manner to facilitate reference and updating by auditors during subsequent audit projects. Again this maintenance function is one that PO should undertake.

The benefits of undertaking project risk audits include:

- Identifying poorly defined contracts and service level agreements
- Identifying poorly defined project management processes
- Identifying poorly defined project objectives
- Identifying poorly defined project deliverables
- Identifying unrealistic project plans
- Identifying unrealistic project expectations
- Identifying overly complex project and resource structures
- Identifying inappropriate product and work breakdown structures
- Identifying unrealistic estimates
- Identifying inadequate standards and procedures
- Identifying inadequate quality documentation
- Identifying inadequate design documentation
- Identifying inadequate source code
- Identifying inadequate testing procedures
- Identifying inadequate migration and transition plans
- Identifying inadequate implementation plans
- Identifying inadequately trained staff
- Identifying inadequate financial controls
- Identifying inadequate channels of communication
- Providing positive feedback on issues and concerns.

5.5 Risk support tools

The ability to effectively communicate risk issues to management is a key function of the risk analysis/assessment tool. It should be able to take advantage of contemporary desktop publishing tools, as well as generating well-presented risk modelling reports completely within the tool's internal resources. These features must effectively illustrate and describe the risks to support sound management decision making for risk management. This function should assemble the information provided, as well as all calculated information, and generate a variety of reports. These reports should include the following:

1 An executive summary including:

- The project problem statement and objective(s)
- Scope and constraints
- An overview of the approach
- Key vulnerabilities and their significance
- Graphic risk illustration at an executive level of integration
- General recommendations

2 An intermediate decision support report – this report should provide decision-making management (and other interested parties) information needed to make well-informed and defensible decisions regarding the purchase and/or development and implementation of safeguard measures. Included should be:

- Introduction. Problem statement, objectives, scope and constraints, and rationale for recommendations as entered originally in the project sizing function.
- Graphic risk models, threat perspective. For each threat there should be a graphic or set of graphic risk illustrations, and later (after risk mitigation analysis) representing selected and recommended safeguards and their combined mitigating effect on an annualized basis.
- Graphic risk models, safeguard perspective. For each suggested safeguard/control, there should be a graphic or set of graphic risk illustrations combining the effect of the safeguard/control for all affected threats on an annualized basis.
- Asset inventory summary. A list of assets and associated values summarized by asset category should be presented.
- Ranked threats lists. A list of all threats identified in the assessment before safeguards/controls are applied should be provided. The same threat list should be resequenced as

appropriate after safeguards/controls are applied to reflect the expected result.

- Detailed vulnerabilities. There should be a facility to support a user-generated narrative interpreting the potential consequence of detected vulnerabilities as desired. Even the most advanced expert system will be enhanced by the experience and insight of the analyst conducting the risk analysis/assessment and his/her ability to analyse and articulate the meaning and consequences of the risk model(s).
- Detailed recommendations. There should be a facility to support a user-generated narrative detailing the safeguard/control recommendations as desired.

3 A technical analysis report – this report should provide all the information, fully detailed, that was generated by and supported the execution of a tool-supported risk analysis/assessment.

- Detailed inventory. A detailed asset inventory organized by category.
- Threat/vulnerability summary. A brief discussion of each vulnerability and associated threat(s) identified in the analysis before and after safeguards are applied.
- Threats and loss analysis. A list of all threats and identification of those threats having the potential for impacting the subject information systems environment, based on the results of the threat/vulnerability analysis and associated threat/vulnerability mapping tasks. The assets potentially impacted by each threat should also be identified here along with the associated SLE and exposure factor data.
- Safeguards selection and cost–benefit analysis. There should be a correlation of vulnerabilities with applicable threats and a detailed analysis of that information for each selected safeguard. The tool should also support present value and return on investment analysis of the selected safeguards/controls.

5.5.1 Cost and benefit

The tool should enable a value-added, profit centre approach to risk management. The tool should be able to support the evaluation of the cost–benefit and effectiveness of existing safeguards and identify savings to be gained with demonstrably cost-effective support of security budgets. It should also support the ability to conduct trend analysis to illustrate the overall effectiveness of applied risk management decision making.

Money spent mitigating qualitatively perceived risk is often found not to be justified by a quantitative risk analysis/assessment.

The tool should enable users to monitor the cost, frequency, and annualized monetary impact of many threats (operator/programming errors, misuse/abuse of resources, inadequate maintenance, natural disasters, etc.) based on generally accepted data and site-specific experience. This analysis helps reduce costs resulting from inadequate or unwarranted controls and increases operating efficiency (Ozier 1999).

5.6 Self-assessment checklist

Ask yourself	Yes	No	Not sure
Monitoring and tracking risk			
• Is the process for monitoring risk clearly defined in the risk management plan?	❏	❏	❏
• Is the frequency for monitoring risk defined in the risk management plan?	❏	❏	❏
• Is the process for monitoring risk adequate and have responsibilities been clearly defined?	❏	❏	❏
• Does the monitoring process have adequately built-in safeguards (that is checks and balances)?	❏	❏	❏
• Do the personnel charged with monitoring and tracking risk have a clear understanding of risk?	❏	❏	❏
• Have the key risk deliverables been identified and approved?	❏	❏	❏
• Have key risk indicators been identified, communicated and implemented?	❏	❏	❏
• Have the top 10 risks for monitoring and tracking been identified?	❏	❏	❏
• Has the project set up a risk database (or risk register)?	❏	❏	❏
• Have personnel been trained to use it?	❏	❏	❏
• Has a regime for risk reporting been set up?	❏	❏	❏
• Has the reporting regime been communicated to all key personnel or project stakeholders?	❏	❏	❏
• Has a project office been established to monitor and track risks?	❏	❏	❏
• Are local risk co-ordinators (LRC) aware of their obligations on risk reporting?	❏	❏	❏
• Have these LRC been briefed on the reporting regime?	❏	❏	❏
• Has a process been agreed to undertake random risk audits?	❏	❏	❏
• Does the process include a communication plan for reporting good/bad news?	❏	❏	❏
• If risk support tools are being used does the project team have a clear understanding of their role in the monitoring and tracking process?	❏	❏	❏
• Have all key project personnel been trained in the use of the tools?	❏	❏	❏
• Does the tool add value to the risk management process?	❏	❏	❏

Case study

Chaos into success

The business case for adapting project management disciplines to large-scale software development is obvious. The devil is in the details.

Corporate America spends more than $275 billion each year on approximately 200 000 application software development projects. A great many of these projects will fail for lack of skilled project management.

The opportunities for project failure are legion. Large-scale software development efforts today are conducted in complex, distributed IT environments. Development occurs in a fragile matrix of applications, users, customer demands, laws, internal politics, budgets, and project and organizational dependencies that change constantly. Project managers who lack enterprise-wide multi-project planning, control, and tracking tools often find it impossible to comprehend the system as a whole. Underestimating project complexity and ignoring changing requirements are basic reasons why projects fail. Under these conditions, software project management is almost an oxymoron.

Moreover, software today must not just automate processes; it must create business value, by improving customer service or delivering a competitive advantage. Raising the stakes of every large-scale development project is return on investment (ROI): software must have a measurable impact on a company's bottom line.

Finally, urgent multi-project, multi-site projects like Y2K, Euro conversion, ERP, and the rush to the Internet add to the daunting development burden.

For all these reasons, the business case for adapting project management disciplines to large-scale software development is obvious. It's the implementation that's dicey.

Committed to winning

Project management is a process that spans the full life cycle of a project from inception to completion. Its cornerstone tenets are planning, execution, and control of all resources, tasks, and activities necessary to complete a project. Project management is not an isolated activity, but rather a team effort. In the end, project management is about people and process – how work is being performed. The four 'Ps' of project management are: People Performing Perfect Process.

Most team efforts fail because members are not committed to winning. Why are the Yankees the Yankees? Because they have an expectation of winning, not losing. And they have a repeatable process that mitigates failure.

Project management is gaining traction in IT organizations, and the results are encouraging. Failure rates and costs are down, and project success rates are up. Large companies are taking a small approach to project management. Minimization means scaled down features/functions as well as scope minimization. IT organizations are adopting standard project methodologies or building enterprise-level formal project management disciplines. This level of proactivity is quite a change.

For years project failure was simply not discussed. And it certainly was not discussed with the CEO. But 1996 was a watershed year in IT project management, according to Standish surveys. We finally came to acknowledge the cost, size, and scope of the problem. We discovered that there was no silver technology bullet. Technology was neither the problem nor the solution.

The problem – and the solution – lay in people and processes. Valuable lessons had been learned and were being applied to current projects. We learned to develop better processes, to organize teams more effectively, and to deal with problems faster. We developed smaller, less complex projects. Troubled projects were euthanized quickly. With the advent of professional project managers, we learned to mitigate project risk through scope minimization, standard infrastructures, and improved communications. History is replete with examples of ambitious projects that failed. The Standish Group believes that failure is critical to success. Only by examining our mistakes and applying lessons learned can we stem the tide of project failures and enhance our organization's probability of success. Using project management practices, we have begun to do just that.

Project resolution: the five-year view

The body of the five years of The Standish Group CHAOS research, our infamous report including detailed information on IT project success and failure, shows decided improvement in IT project management. Project success rates are up across the board, whilst cost and time overruns are uniformly down.

The best news is that we are learning how to succeed more often. In 1994, only 16 per cent of application development projects met the criteria for success – completed on time, on budget, and with all the features/functions originally specified. By 1998, 26 per cent of projects were successful.

The Standish Group classifies projects into three resolution types:

1 Successful: the project is completed on time and on budget, with all features and functions as originally specified.
2 Challenged: the project is completed and operational, but over budget, over the time estimated, and with fewer features and functions than initially specified.
3 Failed: the project is cancelled before completion.

More projects are turning out successfully in all companies, but improvement has been most dramatic in large companies (over $500 million). For example, in 1994 the chance of a project developed by a Fortune 500 company coming in on time and within budget was 9 per cent. The average cost of a Fortune 500 project then was $2.3 million. In 1998, the chance of that same Fortune 500 project succeeding rose to 24 per cent, and the average project cost fell to $1.2 million.

During the same period, 1994 to 1998, medium sized companies also posted higher project success rates and lower average project costs. In small companies, too, success rates rose, but so did average project costs – by 50 per cent.

The Standish Group believes three factors explain these encouraging results. First is a trend toward smaller application development initiatives (our research has always shown smaller projects are more successful because they inherently reduce confusion, complexity, and cost). The two other factors are better project management and greater use of standard infrastructures.

Smaller projects have another benefit. Because they are easier to manage and contain, smaller projects experience fewer time overruns. CHAOS '98 data shows that from 1994 to 1998, the per cent of applications completed 200 per cent over the estimated completion time fell from 12.3 per cent to 2.5 per cent. Even more impressive, the per cent of applications that took under 20 per cent longer than estimated for completion tripled, from 13.9 per cent to 41.1 per cent.

The cost of failed projects went down from $81 billion in 1995 to an estimated $75 billion in 1998. Even more dramatic was a major shift in cost overruns from $59 billion spent in 1995 to an estimated $22 billion in 1998.

Despite this progress, The Standish Group cautions that challenged and failed projects – and their staggering costs – remain the norm.

The three pillars of success

The Standish Group believes three key metrics can assess a project's success potential: project size, project duration, and team size.

- Project size: size does matter. CHAOS research confirms that small projects are more likely to succeed than large projects. As project costs rise, typically through the addition of features and functions that are rarely or never used, the likelihood of success falls. One school of thought would argue that larger projects with more funding and resources should be more successful and should produce more function. Instead, the reverse appears to be true. Smaller projects tend to be more manageable, and it's usually easier to ensure they meet the CHAOS Ten factors to success.
- Project duration and team size: the smaller the team and shorter the duration of the project, the greater the likelihood of success. Obviously, this does not suggest that compressing the schedule and reducing the resources of a large project will make it successful. Nor should it be construed that large projects with large teams cannot be successful. Standish believes that any project can be successful if all the key criteria are met.

We have long been convinced that shorter timeframes, with delivery of software components early and often, increase the success rate. Shorter timeframes foster an iterative process of design, prototype, develop, test, and deploy small elements. 'Growing' (instead of 'developing') software engages the user earlier and confers ownership. And because each software component has a clear and precise statement and set of objectives, realistic user expectations are set.

Certain industries breed success. The Standish Group CHAOS research shows that in 1998 the retail industry had the highest rate of project success (59 per cent) – almost twice the success rate of the financial sector (32 per cent), more than twice that of the manufacturing sector (27 per cent), and three times that of government projects (18 per cent). Of all industries, retail also had the fewest challenged projects (28 per cent) and failed projects (12 per cent).

We believe the retail project success rate is a function of that industry's tight cost controls. The low margin retail industry cannot tolerate waste. The government, on the other hand, has no such challenge.

Company size does not guarantee success. The Standish Group has found no correlation between a company's size and its project success rate. As with project size, bigger is not necessarily better. Whilst large companies (over $500 million) do experience more failures and fewer successes than medium sized companies ($200 million to $500 million), project failure rates generally were distributed quite uniformly across companies of all sizes. Project failure is everyone's problem.

Another way to look at project resolution is by comparing the value of successful projects with the waste of challenged and failed ones. (Value equals money paid for results.)

Along with improvements in time and cost overruns, companies' waste-to-value ratios have improved substantially. In 1996, CHAOS research found 50 per cent waste in IT projects. By 1998 the data identified only 37 per cent waste.

The role of project manager

The IT community is just beginning to understand the true role of the project manager, the skill required to be a good project manager, and the benefits a project manager can bring to any project.

Standish research clearly shows that projects are likely to be less challenged and more successful with a competent and experienced project manager on board. Benefits include reduced project expense, higher company morale, and quicker time to market. The skills most CIOs cite as desirable in a project manager include technology and business knowledge, judgement, negotiation, good communication, and organization. Emphasis is on business skills rather than technical credentials. Moreover, project managers must know not only the business needs of their own company but also those of suppliers and partners. Many of the CIOs we interviewed said that the best IT people make the worst project managers.

In the skills area of project management, the focus is on softer skills, such as diplomacy and time management. Understanding the business is more important than understanding technology; and good communications and writing ability also heads the skills list.

Some project managers can have difficulty dealing with the fact that they seldom have the authority to command resources as required; instead, they must negotiate with the function rep for his or her co-operation. Unless there is a political advantage for the function rep, this can be a hurdle to effective project management. Thus, an investment in a Dale Carnegie course can return a bigger dividend than the latest technology class. The project manager should be 'multilingual', with the skills necessary to converse with all the stakeholders and technical teams. The project manager needs to have a view of the project resources, and how they come together. Giving the project manager exposure throughout the organization will encourage 'multilingual' skills.

Many CIOs confide that their best project managers came with softer skills from outside the IT organization. There must be a core of experienced and competent project managers as role models within the organization. More exposure to both the business organization and the technical teams will increase the project manager's skills. One way to do this is to establish a mentoring and buddy system. Another way is to have monthly brainstorming sessions with just the project managers to exchange ideas and problem resolutions. Project management should be considered a profession, not a discrete task.

The project manager should also be a 'Gatekeeper,' with the authority to decide at the detail level what features and functions will be part of the project. There must be a change policy procedure in place, with associated risk factors and cost increases. Change increases the scope of the project, the time involved, and the chance of failure. The project manager should advise the stakeholders about the risks of scope creep. Since the project manager must orchestrate all the resources so they play together like a fine symphony, he or she must be a 'maestro'. In this regard, the project manager needs to know the depth and skills of all the players to prevent wrong notes. The project manager needs to be empowered to acquire and keep the right talent – and get rid of non-contributors. This is a good example of why small projects work better than those with larger teams.

'Cattle driver' is another hat the project manager must wear. He or she must be a hard driver, and be able to focus on the goal and minimize diversions. The project manager should establish accountability, responsibility, and authenticity.

The project manager should also be a good communicator, both verbally and in writing. To encourage these skills, IT management should consider two training venues: Dale Carnegie classes on how to win friends and influence people, and Toastmaster's classes on how to present. The project manager should be encouraged to use the organization's business dialect to keep communication simple. The project manager should use simple words, avoiding IT buzzwords and acronyms.

Don't put on that hat!

Whilst a project manager's role is multifaceted, there are some roles they should not play. For example, the project manager should not be the executive sponsor. The Standish Group believes the surest road to project failure is through the IT organization. Projects are done on behalf of the business organization, and should have firm executive commitment. IT must set down the rules of engagement and clearly define the roles of the stakeholders. The project manager needs to move with the team, whilst getting the project done. The best way to discourage the project manager from becoming the executive sponsor is to have an effective executive sponsor already. The project manager should not be the user or function representative. The Standish Group has seen many cases where the project manager thought he knew more about the organization than the function rep did. In other cases, the project manager thought she knew more about how the organization should run than the function representatives. However, in most cases this is not so. Project managers should be evaluated based on their project management skills. The best way to discourage a project manager from being a function representative is to have strong user representation.

'Santa Claus' is not a good role for the project manager either. Learning to say 'no' is the hardest lesson for many project managers. Sometimes seemingly simple requests can put the project in real peril. Each feature and function must be measured against business value, project quality, resources, risk, and the schedule. With 80 per cent of delivered features and functions ultimately unused, enlarging the project's scope should not be taken lightly.

The project manager should not be a 'control freak'. Whilst the project manager must control the resources and know all the project details, he or she cannot look over the shoulders of the other stakeholders. Establishing peer review processes, setting and focusing on goals, and having status communications of both meetings and reports can discourage a control freak.

Finally, the project manager cannot be a 'superman'. Even a remarkable project manager cannot save a failing project. It takes all the stakeholders to create a successful project. Setting correct expectations early in the project can have a positive effect. Minimizing project scope will result in a better estimate. Discourage overpromising. A happy stakeholder will be one who is overdelivered.

A project manager is much like a head chef. The Standish Group's recipe for success combines reducing requirements to the very stark minimum, providing constant communication, and coupling that with a standard infrastructure. A good project manager will mix these ingredients with an iterative development process, and project management tools. Bake no longer than six months with six people and success is on the way.

Jim Johnson is chairman of The Standish Group International Inc., Dennis, Mass. The Standish Group specializes in primary research for developing, deploying, and maintaining mission-critical applications.

Project resolution history

	Succeed	Failed	Challenged
1998	26%	28%	46%
1996	27%	40%	33%
1994	16%	31%	53%

(Source: The Standish Group)

Project success rates rise, costs fall (1994 vs 1998)

Company size	Success rate '94	Success rate '98	Project cost '94	Project cost '98	True delta
Large	9%	24%	$2.3M	$1.2M	−65%
Medium	16%	28%	$1.3M	$1.1M	−41%
Small	28%	32%	$0.4M	$0.6M	−4%

Success by project size

Over $10M	0%
$6M to $10M	8%
$3M to $6M	15%
$1.5M to $3M	25%
$750K to $1.5M	33%
Less than $750K	55%

(Source: The Standish Group)

Project duration and team size directly affect project success

Project size	People	Time (months)	Success rate
Less than $750K	6	6	55%
$750K to $1.5M	12	9	33%
$1.5M to $3M	25	12	25%
$3M to $6M	40	18	15%
$6M to $10M	+250	+24	8%
Over $10M	+500	+36	0%

(Source: The Standish Group)

Project complexity heats up

Leveraging workforce availability and skills across multiple projects and geographical boundaries requires an integrated set of tools.

Managing a diversity of skills over multiple projects, simultaneously, is a challenge for executives who are driven to do more with less. However, delivery requirements do not always support using people as efficiently as possible, and project managers face constant time constraints.

This simple paradox raises a new level of complexity for those executives responsible for organizational performance. With staff spread around the world, and increasingly working from home, a cell phone, or the customer's site, success doesn't depend on how a single project is run, but rather, how the workforce executes effective, repeatable, project delivery process.

Static, one-dimensional plans consisting of project schedules are insufficient for today's business needs. Leveraging workforce availability and skills across multiple projects and geographical boundaries requires an integrated set of tools that attack project management trials and tribulations: selecting the right projects; getting them organized; finding the right people; developing accurate estimates; and assigning priority and managing change – overall a hellish task.

Lowering the heat

Multidimensional project management tools can help lower the heat project managers feel. One such tool is Version 6.0 of PlanView Web Software for project and workforce management from PlanView Inc., Austin, Texas. A dynamic, multidimensional tool for resource and programme management, PlanView Web Software is targeted at organizations looking for a common, organizational project delivery process to better manage the work and the workforce. PlanView Software was designed for all managers, including those with little or no project management experience. Executives, customers, and staff working on projects can use the software's capabilities effectively with minimal training – a heavenly thought.

When purchasing such tools as PlanView, organizations must consider these factors:

- Ease of use
- How well the tool supports the end-to-end business process
- What organizational roles are enabled
- The project life cycle
- The application services provided.

PlanView Web Software is a role-based enterprise project and resource management environment delivered to the desktop via a web browser interface. It presents a project delivery model that can be customized to help organizations define and automate key business processes. PlanView Web Software goes beyond traditional project management products to incorporate the informational needs of the broader business organization and related work processes: business development, resource management, project/engagement management, accounting, process/practice management, and knowledge management.

In the PlanView approach, each project follows a consistent work management model representing the project life cycle: Start Work, Plan Work, Plan Resources, Status Work, and Close Work. The PlanView project life cycle can be customized to adapt to specific organizational requirements.

PlanView has a server-centric software architecture that captures critical business logic at the organizational level. Through this architecture, PlanView delivers enterprise services used for planning, interaction, communication, and reporting. Senior managers, project team members, other managers, and even customers are updated in realtime on project changes. PlanView Web Software relies on an industry standard SQL DBMS to manage and store project and workforce information. Both clients and servers run on industry standard hardware and system software platforms, ensuring appropriate standards for compatibility, performance, security, reliability, maintenance, and consistency. This architecture also assures a scalable platform.

The project delivery process

Mature project organizations recognize the role of an integrated project delivery process to:

- Co-ordinate the activities of the project with other affected groups
- Identify and manage resource requirements for today and the future
- Manage organizational knowledge and share project best practices.

Organizations must consider the implications of implementing enterprise-wide planning tools for the business processes currently in place. The diagram below characterizes the work procedures for delivering value to the customer within the typical organization.

PlanView Web Software provides a process framework to help an organization create a project delivery process. Work products produced within PlanView support the performance of these procedures.

By providing information about the workforce capacity, current and forecasted workload organized by work type, client, contract product line, and other attributes important to the organization, PlanView Web Software supports the sales and proposal process.

PlanView also provides workforce development, recruiting, and allocation for approved and pipelined projects, and resource management driven by new business planning and forecasting. PlanView Web Software supports full project/engagement management functionality with server-centric resource planning, estimating, scheduling, and reporting capabilities.

PlanView Software offers a progress engine to support the accounting process. This operation is the collection of effort and expense information to drive billing. Work progress and other financial performance reporting are mandated by business requirements. By utilizing consistent project life cycles and measuring performance, organizations have the information to identify best practices. New standards and methodologies, incorporating best practices, can be established with supporting procedures and templates. Structured and unstructured knowledge can be captured and shared amongst other processes to leverage organizational and staff capability.

Each organization has its own terminology and workflow in its project delivery process. PlanView helps organizations explicitly define their process within the software. Organizational roles then have distinct responsibilities within the process architecture. Properly implemented, the result is repeatable processes with clear accountability – sounds more heavenly all the time.

Personalized web portal

PlanView delivers functionality to users through the HomeView™ portal, which is dynamically built to display software (FeatureSets™) reflecting unique rights, privileges, and access to the central repository. HomeView allows users to personalize their environment by setting their reminders and saving favourite web links, giving them access to discussion groups, and shared development tools and methodologies. Each HomeView portal enables the user to accomplish specific assigned tasks and activities.

Some of the activities performed within PlanView include:

- Manage portfolio – monitor project and resource portfolio performance, authorize resources and budget.

- Manage work – plan work, model, and assign resources; develop estimates and schedules.
- Administer resources – track staff attributes and assignments, model workforce, and approve status reports.
- Exchange work – import/export work products and data between PlanView and other systems, such as Microsoft Project, Oracle Project, or Computron TEAM.
- Submit and approve status – submit, review, and approve status of effort expended and remaining, as well as associated expenses.
- Reports – formulate and distribute both standard and custom reports.
- Administer application – administer users, passwords, common work attributes, and other software parameters.

PlanView Web Software comes with standard roles and defined responsibilities. Users customize these roles to meet specific organizational constructs, and assign individuals to perform specific roles. Standard roles delivered with the PlanView product include:

- Stakeholders – can authorize new work, allocate budget, status existing work, shift work priority, and produce management reports.
- Managers – can plan and schedule work, allocate budgets; search for qualified resources, assign resources, update staff attributes, schedule standard activities (such as vacations), approve timesheets and project status, and produce management reports. Often organizations will subdivide the manager's role into groupings such as project, resource, or service.
- Contributors – are responsible for reporting status, expenses incurred, and time remaining on work performed. Optionally, they can be authorized to accept/decline new work, update their own attributes, and schedule their own standard activities. A contributor can also be granted supervisory responsibilities that allow them to approve the status submitted by others.
- Application administrators – are responsible for establishing and maintaining tables, as well as administering the PlanView software system. They add new users, maintain security and authorizations, and help maintain PlanView data.

Organizations will use these roles as models to define their own roles to include other managers or employees within the enterprise, as well as vendors, partners, service providers, and customers representing the extended enterprise.

PlanView incorporates four planning engines. Managers and others use the Critical Path Engine to calculate the critical path of the project based on priority, standard constraint dates, and relationships. They use the Resource Search Engine to locate people who have the right skills and other criteria and are available to work on their project. A Resource Scheduling Engine calculates resource schedules given existing availability and commitments. A Progressing Engine updates the central repository with results of the project status data to progress schedules, and build earned value and schedule maturity information across the organization.

For organizations with existing investments in project planning software, PlanView provides an application programming interface (API) and integration with Microsoft Project. Projects can be transferred back and forth with other tools, with PlanView used as a central resource pool. Existing competencies can be leveraged and investments in training protected in the Plan-View environment. PlanView also offers an e-mail interface, web access, document attachments, and direct updates to the repository as gateways to support broad collaboration and information sharing, and access to the central repository. Finally, the PlanView server-based Report Engines are available within PlanView to produce individual, project, and organizational reports.

The cost of improvement

PlanView Web Software for project and workforce management, Version 6.0, represents a new generation of capability for individuals responsible for managing multiple projects across geographic boundaries. It is a comprehensive update to Plan-View Version 5.3, extending the product from workforce management to an integrated project and workforce management system. PlanView has accomplished this by improving the user interface, making significant enhancements to the planning and management capability, integrating role definitions in the software, and improving interoperability with other applications. The web-based user interface makes the application accessible and easy to use.

For organizations trying to hold managers accountable for the effective and efficient use of resources on projects for which they are responsible, PlanView provides the ability to monitor and measure performance consistently. Projects and staff can be grouped into various portfolios and compared with peers and the overall performance of the workforce.

PlanView 6.0 is already in use at several organizations. The organizations contacted by The Standish Group told us that their fundamental business rationale for PlanView is to leverage key skills and competencies across the enterprise, understand current and forecasted capacity, and improve project management capability. They all recognized that these improvements come with a cost: investments in the tool, training, management attention, implementation and support, and lost productivity. However, users report these costs to be minimal. They claim that PlanView has delivered an application that can be implemented 'out-of-the-box', is highly configurable, scalable, and easy to use.

These users advise that new businesses choosing PlanView must be open to process and organizational change with respect to the way work is structured and managed, and the way resources are evaluated and assigned. They also highlight the need for implementation planning, including the systems architecture, network capacity, and security.

Finally, these users identified some key challenges facing PlanView: higher level capabilities for resource management and levelling; comparing actual to contracted; and distributing the central repository across multiple locations in the enterprise. They would also like to see web security enhanced.

Hell may have plenty of vacancies for doomed projects, but PlanView Web Software, and other tools like it, may help you reserve your place in heaven.

Project management in cyberspace

Despite hurdles like 'scope creep' CIOs find project management adaptable to virtual teams. As a ubiquitous communications infrastructure, the Internet enables enterprise-wide project management and, soon, the building of virtual project teams within a global, collaborative project management environment.

Because the Internet is the only widely available platform for accessing process and project information, it is a cost-effective backbone for extending project planning and execution to every corporate location using the TCP/IP common denominator. A number of project managers are tapping the power of the Internet and corporate extranets to provide all stakeholders with instant access to project plans, status reports, and meeting minutes.

But project management on a global scale will not be easy.

Most project management techniques were designed for co-located project teams. Those techniques may prove ineffective in global, multisite organizations where members of a project team can be scattered around the world.

Globally distributed software development projects must contend with different languages, cultures, time zones, work ethics, legal systems, and hardware and software requirements. The development of large software systems will require larger teams of people with different knowledge and educational backgrounds to work together at many locations to fulfil the business needs. This fact of life must somehow be weighed against CHAOS findings that project size and scope creep threaten project success.

How to co-ordinate and manage the work of geographically distributed high-performance virtual project teams, how to provide global access to project plans and dynamic project data, and how to internalize the experience of past projects to make it usable for future projects are challenges to be addressed. In addition, configuration management systems that maintain several versions of a system for an orderly development process must be extended for the virtual environment of globally distributed teams.

Despite the hurdles, recent Standish Group research found that project management is one process cited by CIOs as most adaptable to virtual environments.

CIOs understand that managing a virtual project workforce is not technology dependent. From e-mail to cell phones and pagers, communication abounds. The heart of project management is people and processes, not tools and technology.

CHAOS University participants engaged in building or supporting virtual enterprises report that the top three cyberworker issues are measuring productivity, managing communications, and motivating isolated workers.

Project size magnifies these human challenges. Building virtual teams with a minimum of face time, clearly defining work, measuring worker productivity, and managing employee communications across time zones are the chief management priorities.

(This case study first appeared in *Software Magazine* in December 1999 as 'CHAOS into Success' by Jim Johnson and is reproduced by kind permission of the publisher Wiesner Publications, Inc. and the editorial director John P. Desmond. Copyright © 1999–2002 *Software Magazine* and Wiesner Publishing.)

Appendix A
Glossary of risk terminology

Assumption analysis   A three stage process facilitating rapid assessment of impact and stability of assumptions affecting a project.

Brainstorming   An intense and focused scrutiny of an issue with the aim of covering it as intensively as possible. Uses creative and lateral thinking to identify as many possibilities as possible and structured analysis to select suitable options.

Business continuity planning   Contingency plans which deal with the potential impact of risks so severe that they threaten the continuity of the business.

Cause-and-effect analysis   A method of representing the causes and consequences of a risk so that the likelihood and impact may be more accurately calculated. A combination of a fault tree and event tree.

Chance   The potential for the occurrence of an event or the outcome of an uncertainty.

Checklist   A list of closed (yes/no) questions to allow consideration of risks based on previous experience.

Confidence levels   A range of outcomes within which one is confident that a result will occur to a given level of probability.

Contingency   Provision of a margin (for example, within the funds available for the project, the time available for project delivery, or in overspecification of product characteristics) so that project achievement may be optimized against the project objectives in the face of risk impact – allowing for the cost and opportunity cost of the margin.

Corporate governance   The consolidation of a number of reports that define good practice for companies (specifically those listed on the London Stock Exchange).

Criticality   Correlation between a task duration and the overall end date. The effect that the activity has on the project finish.

Criticality index   An index representing the likelihood that an activity will be on the critical path.

Cumulative probability curve   The output of a Monte Carlo simulation which shows the probability of delivering a project within a chosen limit. Sometimes called an 'S' curve due to its characteristic shape.

Decision tree   A branch-like representation of the alternative courses of action available when making a decision.

Delphi technique   A process where a consensus view is reached by consultation with a number of independent experts, eventually reconciled to one conclusion. Often used as an estimating technique.

Fallback plan   Plan for an alternative course of action that can be adopted to overcome the consequences of the risk should it occur. Also called contingency plan.

Flowcharting   A graphical representation of a process flow.

Focused interview   Interview with a project team member carried out in a structured method in order to elicit specific information about risks. Also called a structured interview – often uses a prompt list.

Hazard   An existing condition which may result in an unfavourable outcome.

Impact   A measure of risk consequence.

Likelihood   A measure of the chance that a risk might occur. Measured either as a probability that the risk will occur, or the frequency with which the risk might occur during a specific time period.

Impact matrix   A matrix with likelihood on one or more axis and impact on the other. The body of the matrix has an assessment of the risk priority.

Monte Carlo simulation   A quantitative risk assessment method. Determines the possible range of outcomes by using random numbers to create one possible outcome, and repeating many times using different random numbers.

Net present value (NPV)   A method of calculating the worth of future income/expenditure streams. Based on the premise that future money is worth less than today.

Objectives analysis   A method of clarifying objectives of a project.

Opportunity   A risk where the potential outcome is beneficial to the project or business objective.

Probability   Chance that an event will occur, measured between 0 (impossible) and 1 (likely).

Probability distribution   A description of the possible values that a variable may take. Can describe the uncertainty or variability of an activity in terms of duration.

Prompt list   A list of open questions used in risk identification to direct through to particular areas.

Qualitative risk assessment   Methods of prioritizing risk without quantifying them.

Quantitative risk assessment   Methods of assessing numerically the overall effect of risks on the project objectives, usually on the project cost and/or schedule.

Risk analysis   The use of available information to characterize risks.

Risk assessment   The process of evaluating an identified risk.

Risk avoidance   Changing project objectives or methods to avoid the possibility of the risk occurring.

Risk behaviour   The response of an individual to perceived risks. Different people may react differently to the same risk, or the attitude of a person may be different at various times. The response may be affected by a number of different factors.

Risk consequence   The outcome of a risk if it should occur.

Risk control   Selection and implementation of appropriate options for dealing with risk.

Risk evaluation   Process used to decide risk management priorities by evaluating and comparing the level of risk against predetermined standards, target risk levels or other criteria.

Risk identification   Determination of what could pose a risk.

Risk management   Systematic application of policies, procedures, methods, and practices to the task of identifying assessing, planning and managing risk.

Risk management plan   A document defining how risk management is to be implemented in the context of a particular project.

Risk mitigation   Action either to reduce the probability of an adverse event occurring or to reduce the consequences if it does occur.

Risk prioritizing   Ordering of risks according to their risk value, and then by which risks need to be considered for risk reduction, risk avoidance and risk transfer.

Risk quantification   Process of applying values to the various aspects of risk.

Risk ranking   Allocating a classification to the impact and likelihood of a risk.

Risk register   The formal record of identified risks. A body of information listing all risks identified for the project, explaining the nature of each risk and recording information relevant to its assessment and management.

Risk sharing   Spreading of risk by sharing it with others. Does not reduce the risk, but encourages others to take an interest in reducing the risk, and spreads the consequences of the risk occurring.

Secondary risk   A risk that may occur as a result of invoking a risk response or fallback plan. Risk arising from risk treatment process. Also known as consequential risk.

Sensitivity analysis   An analysis of the effect on the objectives of the project or business of changing a particular value.

Stakeholder   Individual, group or organization having a vested interest or influence on the business or project.

Stakeholder analysis   Process for identifying stakeholders, their interests and influence.

Strategic risk   Risk to goals, objectives or stakeholders.

SWOT analysis   A process identifying the Strengths, Weaknesses, Opportunities and Threats present.

Threat   A risk with a potential harmful outcome.

Uncertainty   A state of incomplete knowledge about some item.

Variability risk   The inherent uncertainty (in cost or duration) in a planned activity. The range of values that the activity may take expressed as a probability distribution.

Variance   A measure of the width of a probability distribution. The square root of the variance is called the standard deviation.

Product	Web site	Classification
@RISK for Microsoft Project	www.palisade-europe.com	Simulation tool
Active Risk Manager	www.strategicthought.co.uk	Risk status monitor
Analytica	www.lumina.com	Simulation tool
CRIMS	www.expertchoice.com	Decision support tool
CRYSTALL BALL	www.rmg.co.uk	Simulation tool
Decision Pro	www.vangaurdesw.com	Decision support
Designsafe	www.designsafe.com	Risk tool kit
DMT	www.dependency.com	Decision support tool
DPL	www.adainc.com	Decision support tool
Futura	www.futura-da.fi.com	Risk tool kit
Goldsim	www.goldsim.com	Simulation tool
IDecide	www.decisivetools.com	Decision support tool
Mesa/Vista Risk Manager	www.mesasys.com	Generic risk tool
Monte Carlo	www.primavera.com	Simulation tool
NicklebyKit	www.nickleby.com	Generic risk tool
OpenPlan Professional	www.welcom.com	Generic risk tool
PANDORA	www.bmtrcl.com	Generic risk tool
Panorama PSA	www.panorama.com	Generic risk tool
Pertmaster Professional + Risk	www.pertmaster.com	Simulation tool
PHA-Pro 5	www.dyadem.com	Generic risk tool
Powersim Solver	www.powersim.com	Generic risk tool
PRA	www.users.lia.net/katmar	Simulation tool
Precision Tree	www.palisade-europe.com	Decision support tool

Product	Web site	Classification
Predict Risk Analyser	www.riskdecisions.com	Simulation tool
Predict Risk Controller	www.riskdecision.com	Generic risk tool
ProAct	www.rcinc.com	Generic risk tool
Project Self-Assessment Kit	www.klci.com	Risk measurement tool
REMIS	www.hvr-csl.co.uk	Generic risk tool
Ris3/RisGen	www.ris3.com	Generic risk tool
Risk in Action	www.adacel.co.uk	Risk analysis tool
Risk Matrix	www.mitre.org	Generic risk tool
Risk Maturity Model	www.hvr-csl.co.uk	Generic risk tool
Risk Radar	www.spmn.com	Generic risk tool
Risk +	www.proj-ini.co.uk	Simulation tool
Risk Com	www.ciria.org.uk	Generic risk tool
RiskEZ	www.pinyonsoftware.com	Generic risk tool
RiskFolio	www.risklabs.com	Risk management tool
Risk Safe	www.dyadem.com	Generic risk tool
Risk Tools	www.risk-reward.com	Decision support tool
Risk Trak	www.stgrp.com	Generic risk tool
SCRAM	www.scramsoftware.vallnet.com	Generic risk tool
SmartRISK	www.uspioneer.com	Generic risk tool
SRE	www.sei.edu	Decision support tool
STRAD	www.btinternet.com	Decision support tool
TDRM	www.hvr-csl.co.uk	Risk identification kit
TRAM 2000	www.hvr-csl.co.uk	Risk analysis tool

Boehm, B.W. and Ross, R., 'Theory-W Software Project Management: Principles and Examples', *IEEE Trans. Software Engineering*, Vol. 15, No. 7, 902–916, 1989.

Boehm, B.W., 'Software Risk Management: Principles and Practices', *IEEE Software*, January, 32–41, 1991.

Boehm, B.W. and DeMarco, T., 'Software Risk Management', *IEEE Software*, May/June 1997, 17–19.

Briand, L.C., Thomas, W.M. and Hetmanski, C.J., 'Modeling and Managing Risk Early in Software Development', 15th International Conference on Software Engineering, Ch. 46, pp 55–65.

Bustard, D.W., Greer, D. and Tate, G., 'Enhancing Soft Systems Methodology with Risk Management Techniques', in *Software Quality Management II*, Vol. 2, Ch. 53, 145–147, Elsevier, Southampton, 1994.

Carr, M.L., Konda, S.L., Monarch, I., Ulrich, F.C. and Walker, C.F., 'Taxonomy-Based Risk Identification', Technical Report CMU/SEI-93-TR-6, Software Eng. Inst., Carnegie-Mellon University, Pittsburg, PA, 15213, USA, 1993.

Carter, B., Hancock, T., Morin, J. and Robins, N., *Introducing Riskman Methodology*, NCC Blackwell, 1994.

CCTA (Central Communications and Telecommunications Agency – UK Civil Service), *Introduction to the Management of Risk*, HMSO Books, London, 1993.

CCTA, *Management of Risk*, Prince 2, Ch. 8, pp. 55–60.

Charette, R., *Software Engineering Risk Analysis and Management*, McGraw-Hill, NY, 1989.

Charette, R., 'Essential Risk Management: Notes from the Front', Proceedings of the 2nd SEI Conference on Software Risk, 1993.

Charette, R., 'How to Create a Successful Failure', *Communications of the ACM*, Vol. 38, No. 5, 122, May 1995.

Charette, R., Adams, K.M. and White, M.B., 'Managing Risk in Software Maintenance', *IEEE Software*, May/June 1997, 43–50.

Down, A., Coleman, M. and Absalon, P., *Risk Management for Software Projects*, McGraw-Hill, London, 1994.

Dorofee, A.J., Walker, J., Alberts, C.J., Higuera, R.P., Murphy, R.L. and Williams, R.C., *Continuous Risk Management Guidebook*, Carnegie Mellon University, SEI, 1996.

Fairley, R., 'Risk Management for Software Projects', *IEEE Software*, Vol. 11, No. 3, 57–67, 1994.

Gluch, D.P., 'A Construct for Describing Software Risks', Software Engineering Institute Technical Report CMU/SEI-94-TR-14, SEI, Pittsburgh, PA, July 1994.

Garvey, P., Phair, D.J. and Wilson, J.A., 'An Information Architecture for Risk Assessment and Management', *IEEE Software*, May/June 1997, 25–35.

Greer, D. and Bustard, D.W., 'Towards an Evolutionary Delivery Strategy based on Risk Analysis', Proceedings of Engineering of Computer Based Systems, IEEE Computer Society Press, March 1996.

Hall, E.M., *Managing Risk: Methods for Software Systems Development*, SEI series in Software Engineering, Addison-Wesley, 1998.

Lyytinen, K., Mathiassen, L. and Ropponen, J., 'A Framework for Software Risk Management', *Journal of Information Technology*, Vol. 11, No. 4, 275–285, 1996.

Madachy, R.J., 'Heuristic Risk Assessment using Cost Factors', *IEEE Software*, May/June 1997, 51–59.

Monarch, I. and Gluch, D.P., 'An Experiment in Software Development Risk Information Analysis', Software Engineering Institute, Technical Report: CMU/SEI-95-TR-014; ESC-TR-95–014, October 1995.

Mumford, E., 'Risky Ideas in the Risky Society', *Journal of Information Technology*, 11, 321–331, 1996.

Ould, M.A., *Strategies for Software Engineering: The Management of Risk and Quality*, John Wiley, NY, 1990.

Powell, P.L. and Klein, J.H., 'Risk Management for Information Systems Development', *Journal of Information Technology*, 11, 309–319, 1996.

Phelps, R., 'Risk Management and Agency Theory in IS Projects – An Exploratory Study', *Journal of Information Technology*, 11, 297–307, 1996.

Redmill, F., 'Risk Management is for Everyone part 1', *iText*, Vol. 1, Issue 1, 58–60.

Royal Society, *Risk Analysis, Perception and Management*, Royal Society, London, 1992 (ISBN: 0–85403–467–6).

Rowe, W.D., *An Anatomy of Risk*, Robert E. Krieger Pub Co., FL, 1988.

Sherer, S.A., 'Measuring Software Failure Risk: Methodology and an Example', *Journal of Systems Software*, 25, 257–269, 1994.

Warner, F., *Risk: Analysis, Perception, Management*, pp. 1–12, The Royal Society, London, 1992.

Yau, C., 'A Quantitative Methodology for Software Risk Control', Proceedings of the 1994 IEEE International Conference on Systems, Man and Cybernetics, Vols 1–3, Ch. 493, pp. 2015–2020, 1994.

References

Balint, S. and Nottingham, A. 'A Framework for Analysing Risks Associated with IS/IT Investments', Information Systems Methodologies Conference Proceedings, September 1995.

Boehm, Barry W. 'Software Risk Management: Principles and Practices', *IEEE Software*, January 1991.

Brewer, 1999, Information based on a presentation given by Dr Brewer at the Second Annual Conference of e-Commerce and the supply chain revolution, June 1999.

Cash, J., McFarlan, W. and McKenney, J. *Corporate Information Systems Management*, Irwin, Boston, 1992.

Charette, Robert N. *Software Engineering Risk Analysis and Management*, McGraw-Hill Book Company, New York, 1989.

Clayton Andrew, Oakley Peter and Pratt Brian *Empowering People: A Guide to Participation*, New York: UNDP, 1998.

Cook, D.W. and Seiford, L.M. 'The Borda–Kendall Consensus Method for Priority Ranking Problems', *Management Science*, Vol. 28, pp. 621–637.

de Bakker, Karel, Stewart, Wendy M. and Shermeta, Peter W. 'Risk Management Planning – How Much is Good Enough?' PMI Europe Conference, June 2002, Cannes, France.

Eden, C., Jones, S. and Sims, D. *Thinking in Organisations*, McMillan Press, 1979.

Federal Supplement (1979), *Chatlos Systems v. National Cash Register Corp.*, Vol. 479, p. 738, United States District Court for the District of New Jersey.

Glutch, David P. *A Construct for Describing Software Development Risks*, SEI Carnegie Mellon University, Pittsburgh, Pennsylvania, USA, 1994.

Gonulkiewicz, R. 'The Implied Warranty in Software Contracts', *The John Marshall Journal of Computer & Information Law*, Winter **16**(2), 1997, p. 393.

Goodwin, Steve, (Editor-in-Chief, 'Software Risk Management Makes Good Business Sense'. *SRM Magazine*, Q4 2000).

Haimes, Yacov Y. 'Total Risk Management', *Risk Analysis* **11**(2) pp. 169–171, 1991.

Higuera, Ronald P. and Haimes, Yacov Y. *Software Risk Management*, SEI, 1996.

Kloman, Felix H., Seawreck Press, Inc., September 2001.

McAllister, K. *Understanding Participation: Monitoring and Evaluating Process, Outputs and Outcomes*, Ottawa, IDRC, 1999.

McManus, John 'A Practical Approach to Project Appraisal', *Management Accounting*, November 1981, pp. 38–40.

McManus, John, 'The Influence of Stakeholder Values on Project Management', *Management Services*, June 2002, pp. 8–15.

McManus, John, 'Risk in Software Projects', *Management Services*, October 2001, pp. 6–10.

McNamee, David 'Developing an IS Risk Assessment Process', Mc^2 Management Consulting, 2002. The full case study about developing an IS risk assessment process that integrates well with the rest of the business process, first appeared in the ISACA Journal in 1996. Reproduced with permission.

Ozier, Will ('A Framework for an Automated Risk Assessment Tool', *ITAudit*, Vol. 2, August 1999. Reproduced by permission.)

Porter, M.E. *Competitive Advantage*, Free Press, 1985.

Pressman, Roger S. *Software Engineering, A Practitioner's Approach*, reproduced with permission of Dr James Collofello and Andrew Pinkerton, from their material *Risk Identification in the Classroom*, Arizona State University, USA. Marvin J. Carr *et al.*, *Taxonomy-Based Risk Identification*, 1993, Software Engineering Institute at Carnegie Mellon University, Pittsburgh, Pennsylvania 15213. Roger S. Pressman, *Software Engineering, A Practitioner's Approach*, third edition, 1992.

Pressman, Roger S. 'Understanding Software Engineering Practices: Required at SEI Level 2 Process Maturity', Software Engineering Training Series briefing presented to the Software Engineering Process Group, 30 July 1993.

Rainbow, Roger, 'Control Risks Group', in 'Letters', *The Economist*, 10 November 2001.

Sangster, Alon (ed:) *New Review of Applied Expert Systems*, Taylor Graham Publishing, ISSN: 1361–0244.

Schultz, Steve, APMCP, newsletter, April 2000.

Watts R., *Measuring Software Quality*, NCC, Blackwell Publications, UK, 1987.

Wiegers, Karl, 'Know Your Enemy: Software Risk Management', *Software Development Magazine*, 1998.

Index